kid
V · I · D

FUN-DAMENTALS

OF VIDEO

INSTRUCTION

Grades: 4 through 12

CUT STAND-BY SPEED-UP READY

KAYE BLACK
with illustrations by
GORDON MURRAY

Zephyr
Press ®

REACHING THEIR HIGHEST POTENTIAL

KidVid
Fun-damentals of Video Instruction
Grades: 4 through 12

© 2000 by Zephyr Press
Printed in the United States of America
ISBN 1-56976-104-3

Editing: Susan Newcomer and Stacey Shropshire
Cover design: Kathleen Koopman
Design: Kathleen Koopman
Typesetting: Mo Martin
Illustrations: Gordon Murray

Zephyr Press
P.O. Box 66006
Tucson, Arizona 85728-6006
http://www.zephyrpress.com

ACKNOWLEDGMENT

Thanks to Jo Taylor, Process Video Producer, for her expertise and guidance

Library of Congress Cataloging-in-Publication Data are available.

CONTENTS

VIDEO PRODUCTION IN 9 EASY LESSONS

APPENDIXES

GLOSSARY

INTERNET RESOURCES

BIBLIOGRAPHY

INTRODUCTION

So you want to teach video?

So you want to teach your students to "convert audio and video signals into electronic pulses and record these pulses on electromagnetic tape"? Sounds technical, doesn't it? But is it? Does video have to be technical? Not at all!

Video is used everywhere—at home, in the office, in police departments, theaters, hospitals, banks, stores, libraries, restaurants—even schools! Anything people want to investigate, teach, or recall is, or soon will be, videotaped. Video is a part of the present that will affect the future in ways we haven't even imagined. What possibilities! You can prepare students for this future by getting involved in video now. Video is creative, challenging, and definitely fun! And it can be extremely useful in the daily life of your school.

I started teaching video like most teachers—I knew nothing! I even resisted doing video because I felt technophobic. But when I thought about the impact that video will have on students and their future, I realized that the advantages of doing video far outweigh the disadvantages. So I decided to do video *for them*. And—surprise! We learned together. I learned that teaching video can be fun. By the end of the unit, I was doing video *for me!*

You can teach video to your class, too. With some basic equipment and this guide, you can begin to enjoy and use this important medium.

KIDVID presents a practical learning program to help students understand and use video. They will be doing the writing, the camerawork, the editing. You will simply supervise. The curriculum is designed to be used with upper-elementary school students, but with a little revision, the curriculum can be used with just about any age level.

It's important to remember that as the teacher, you are still the authority figure in the classroom and that you must not only model appropriate behavior and products, but expect them from your students. With this in mind, choose your examples carefully and do not tolerate student work that exhibits undue violence or emphasizes inappropriate behavior without showing consequences or resolutions. You will have students who attempt to focus on silly or immature circumstances. It is your responsibility, then, to insist on more appropriate themes and scripting. You will need to monitor these students closely throughout the entire production process to ensure that it is a positive growth experience for all concerned.

Specifically, **KIDVID** will help students

- recognize the elements that affect the quality of a video production
- develop the analytical skills necessary to interpret relationships among these elements
- construct criteria for evaluating effective video productions
- learn the fundamental techniques of video production, including preproduction planning (using scripts and storyboards) and technical skills (working with the camera and lights, for example); in **KID-VID**, students move quickly from theory to hands-on experience with equipment, and, for them hands-on is the most exciting part

KIDVID is organized into three parts. "The Basics" offers a general introduction to video and basic video equipment. "Production Techniques" introduces the basic skills and terminology you will need to teach video. "Video Production in 9 Easy Lessons" presents a step-by-step guide for teaching video production, from Lesson 1, which invites students to evaluate their favorite television show, to Lesson 9, which asks students to evaluate the video production they have just completed in class! In addition, the appendixes include sample forms, a list of references, material on the many uses of video in the schools, and information on how to prepare instructional material for the classroom. The glossary includes technical terms used in this book.

If you didn't think video was easy before **KIDVID,** you will now! So let's begin . . . 5 . . . 4 . . . 3 . . . 2 . . . 1 . . . Roll tape!

THE BASICS

WHAT IS VIDEO?

Videotape is a thin plastic film covered with a magnetically sensitive coating. Audio and video information is recorded in separate sections (called "tracks") on the tape. When the tape is recording, the camera converts audio and video signals to electrical impulses. These impulses are stored on the videotape as changes in the magnetic coating.

When we think of video, we often think of television. Television has been around for many years (it was actually invented in the early 1900s but perfected much later). Video—the recording of the audio and video images—took longer to develop and is still evolving today.

The first videotape recorder was introduced in the late 1950s and was expensive, cumbersome, and fragile. Many different formats (methods of recording that are incompatible) were competing for the market at first, but finally the market condensed to two basic formats, Beta and VHS (which are still incompatible).

Videotape is *not* film. It does not look, feel, or act like film. Videotape has no frames or sprockets, and it does not need to be threaded, spliced, or touched in any way. It is cheaper than film and provides immediate feedback. It does not need to be developed in a laboratory. It can be stored, erased, and reused, sped up, slowed down, or even paused to "freeze" the action. It is easy to revise, edit, and correct. With one or two pieces of equipment, we can easily show video at home on a standard television set.

> Video/'vid-e-o/n., adj., [L *videre* to see + E -O] 1. being, relating to or used in the transmission or reception of the television image.
>
> video, Latin, *I see*
>
> *Merriam Webster's Collegiate Dictionary,* 10th ed.

THE BASICS

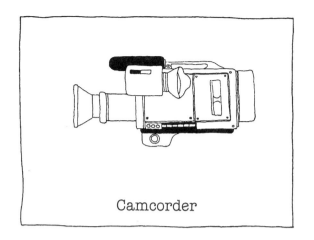

Camcorder

In many cities, local cable companies have public access channels in their broadcast formats. Public access means that individual citizens are granted access to three or four cable television channels to display their own video material. More and more individuals are producing videos. Many cities have set up community cable corporations to give citizens access to equipment, studios, and training. Contact your local television company to find which access options are available in your area.

The prices of both video equipment and supplies continue to fall. Quality and reliability remain high, and features that add special effects are becoming more and more standard.

Video production is becoming easier every day. With a few pieces of equipment and an imaginative mind, anyone can make a video!

But you will need some basic equipment, which is described in the following section.

BASIC EQUIPMENT
Camera or Camcorder

A video camera or camcorder translates light into recorded electronic information. Camcorders usually require a battery pack for power.

Recording videotape with a camcorder is relatively easy. The cameraperson simply points the camera at the scene to be recorded and pushes a button.

Advantages of a Camcorder

- can be operated by one person
- is convenient to use
- needs no cable connectors to VCR
- is portable, not cumbersome
- possibly has many automatic features (white balancing, focus, and so forth)

Disadvantages of a Camcorder
- when one part breaks, the entire camera usually must be replaced
- can be heavy or awkward for students

To use a camcorder correctly, students need to know all its parts. The generic camera illustrated on page 12 may differ from yours, so be sure to refer to the owner's manual for specific parts identification and instructions. I cannot overemphasize this point! Before all else fails, read the instructions!

Video Cassette Recorder (VCR)

A videocassette recorder (VCR), also called a videotape recorder (VTR), records a signal onto videotape and plays the tape back. If you have a camcorder you will not need a VCR for recording. You will be using the VCR only for playing back students' recorded material.

Tripod

A tripod is a three-legged adjustable stand used to hold the camera steady during taping. It often comes with a special plate that screws into a universal slot in the bottom of the camera or camcorder. This plate allows people to attach or remove a camera from the tripod with the flip of a switch. You can purchase the tripod with a *camera head* or *pan head*, a top designed to hold a camera. With this head students can

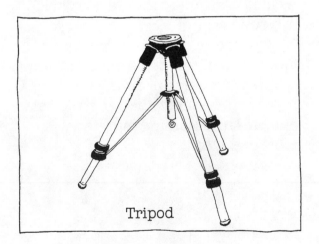

Tripod

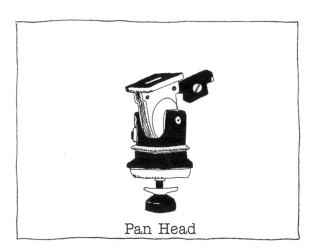

Pan Head

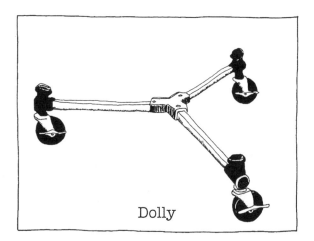

Dolly

Dolly

A dolly is a wheeled rack to which you can attach a tripod. It allows the tripod and camera to be wheeled around smoothly.

Young students can use both tripods and dollies. Unfortunately, better tripods and dollies are more expensive, but the extra investment is worth it. Because young hands are not strong enough to tighten the connections properly, your students will appreciate a good tripod and dolly with their easier-to-tighten connections.

securely lock the camera in position, but they will have little freedom of movement. For greater movement, you can purchase a *video head* (also called a *fluid head* or *fluid effect head*) that will allow students to move the camera smoothly in any direction. You may also purchase a single pole called a *monopod* that screws directly into the bottom of the camera—it doesn't use a head—to steady the camera.

THE BASICS

Parts of the Camcorder

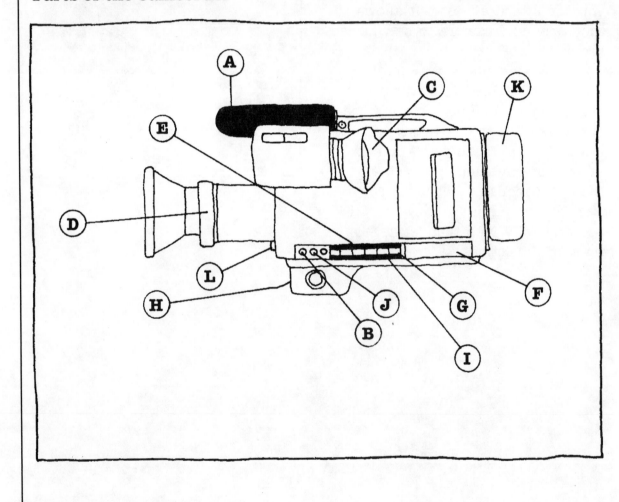

A. **Microphone:** Records sound on the tape. There may also be an input socket for another external mike.

B. **White balance:** Students set this switch when they begin to tape and adjust it when they change lighting (for example, when they move from inside to outside). White balancing tells the camera what "white" is. Many newer models have an automatic white balance function, or claim to! It is best for students to adjust the balance manually if they can. See the camera manual for directions and the section "White Balancing" (page 26).

C. **Viewfinder:** The viewfinder allows the cameraperson to see what he or she is taping, and some models will play back what has been taped for review. It also displays various indicators to tell if the light is adequate for recording, if the battery is charged, and other information. Many models have flip-over LCD monitor viewfinders. Monitors and TVs vary in size and shape, however, so ask students to practice so they can get what they expect on the TV or monitor you have.

D. Lens assembly: The lens assembly handles all the light that comes into the camera. Its construction is similar to that on a still camera. Adding special lenses gets special effects. It is the part of the camera that will focus and zoom. Some expensive cameras have interchangeable lenses for special purposes, such as a long telephoto lens for athletic events.

E. Control panel: These controls enable students to use the camcorder as a VCR (rewind or play the tape back through the monitor, for example).

F. Special effects panel: These controls allow students to include special effects on the tape, such as mosaics, freeze frames, and so on. Check your manual for specific information about your model.

G. Record button: The record button enables students to record and pause during the recording.

H. Zoom toggle button: This two-way button enables students to zoom the camera lens in and out. It is sometimes marked T for telephoto and W for wide angle.

I. Exposure compensation control: This button or dial is used to improve the image in special lighting situations.

J. Battery: Most batteries are rechargeable. You can purchase a larger battery to supply power longer. Some batteries also plug directly into a wall outlet. Batteries must be faithfully recharged after each use!

K. Focus: This button will switch the camera from automatic focus to manual focus. With manual focus, students must focus the lens themselves.

L. Miscellaneous controls: These include buttons to film the date, time of day, and so on.

Microphone

Video cameras record sound as well as pictures. A microphone is often housed inside the camera, and in addition, most cameras have a separate input plug to which an external mike can be attached. Be aware that attaching an external mike will usually cancel the internal one. You must use the right size plug or jack. You can usually purchase plug adapters off the shelf in a local electronics store.

Do not plan to use a separate microphone and tape recorder to record people talking and add audio later because it is almost impossible to match lips to sounds in a video tape.

Lights

A camera simply will not work without light. Light is what is recorded electronically on the videotape. Two types of light are available: natural light and artificial light.

Natural light is an obvious choice for outdoors. Direct sunlight is a strong source, but overhead, it often casts harsh shadows, which keep moving, and sunlight may make subjects squint. To compensate for these drawbacks, students can use reflectors or additional fill lights. Reflectors are white or shiny surfaces that bounce light into certain areas. Students can use them to fill in shadows. Fill lights are simply electric lights that add additional lighting to a scene. Remember that they will need a source of power to work, either a battery or an outlet, and they must be strong or close enough to match the sunlight.

Artificial light can be as simple as a few clip-on "scoop" lights. Available at any hardware store, these inexpensive lights are fine for beginners, but be aware that they will not accept very high wattage (check the lamp, usually rated up to 100 watts). Similar but more heavy-duty scoop lamps will accept up to 500-watt bulbs and can be purchased at any camera store. Do not forget the special tripods available to hold lights. Camera store staff can introduce you to a variety of other lights and lamps, and teach you a lot more about lighting.

Television/Monitor

You must have a television or a monitor to view taped material. The difference between a television and a monitor is this: a standard television receives video and audio signals on a radio frequency through its antenna, whereas a monitor receives signals only through its input connections. Monitors usually accept signals from such sources as VCRs, video cameras, computers, and so forth. Monitors usually provide a better picture because there is no antenna interference, and video signals can be separated from audio signals. Some televisions can be used as monitors, however, so check carefully when you purchase equipment.

CAMCORDER PURCHASING TIPS AND TAPE FORMATS

Camcorders are available in a variety of video formats. Your budget, available equipment, and curriculum will determine what is most practical for you.

Camcorders are often classified based on the type of tape they use. Least expensive are the standard VHS and 8-millimeter (8mm) camcorders. VHS is the more common in schools; most VCRs and editing equipment use this format. But VHS has lower resolution (image detail) and copied tapes are increasingly poor quality due to generation loss.

The 8mm format is currently the most popular consumer choice because it is lightweight and easy to use. Its quality is higher than standard VHS tapes and the tape time is comparable. The high 8 version of 8mm records the tape electronically and at a higher resolution. Both formats are poor choices if you want broadcast-quality productions. *Broadcast-quality* is material that would be good enough to be broadcast, often superior to most home or amateur video.

Other types of camcorders include Super VHS (SVHS) and high 8 formats, which you would use if you want higher-quality results. Super VHS camcorders are more practical than high 8 because you can also use regular VHS tapes in them. However, standard VHS VCRs cannot play high 8, 8mm, and videotapes recorded in SVHS format, and any editing equipment must be specific to that format, as well.

Smaller C ("compact" or "VHSC") formats are also available. These cameras compromise: they have the smaller camera size of the 8mm, but you can play the tapes in a standard VCR with the use of an adapter. These cameras can be difficult to hold steady, and their shorter recording times also produce tapes of lesser quality than the 8mm. Smaller children, though, may find the camera easier to carry and use.

Digital camcorders are new in the format wars. They produce the highest quality; there is no generation loss in editing. These camcorders record onto a digital cassette tape so you need different editing and playback equipment or a

digital video input into your computer. Currently more expensive than other formats, prices are dropping quickly.

Be aware that most manufacturers provide consumer and professional versions of each model. The professional models, though more expensive, are sturdier, more forgiving, and easier for students to use.

Best Camcorder Features to Have

Remember: More features do not necessarily make a better camcorder!! Look for a camcorder that produces the highest-quality video. You may want to check out consumer magazines to see which brands are highly rated.

Once you have found one, though, the following features are definitely worth shopping for:

- both an eyepiece viewfinder and flip screenmonitor
- low lux number (responsiveness to low light)
- 8:1 zoom lens with macro capability (6:1 minimum)
- "flying erase" heads (for smooth edits)
- basic special effects (fade/wipe/titles)
- lightweight construction

Also worth looking for are *digital image stabilization* (also called *image stabilizer*), which holds an image steady while your nervous student shakes the camera. Many models offer digital zoom features, but they compromise quality. A manual focus and iris are great to have.

Helpful Accessories

- camcorder case
- extra batteries
- tripod with dolly wheels
- various types of microphones (shotgun, wireless FM, lapel clip)
- high-intensity spotlight (camera or stand mounted)
- shoulder camera mount
- monopod (one-legged tripod)
- editor/controller
- special effects generator
- audio dub

CARE AND FEEDING OF YOUR EQUIPMENT

Video equipment can be very sensitive to light, moisture, and electrical fields. Be sure everyone using the equipment follows these guidelines to protect it:

- Do not place tapes and equipment where a magnetic field can damage them (on top of a speaker, for example).
- Do not point a camcorder at a light source; although newer camcorders can take direct light sources, why chance it?

Cleaning

Clean the playback and recording heads on your VCR and camcorder regularly. Purchase head-cleaning tapes at any video store. Non-abrasive "wet head" cleaning cartridges cause less wear and give a longer life to your heads. You can also have your heads professionally cleaned.

Batteries

All batteries have a "memory" and should be completely dead before recharging. If you fail to wait until they are completely dead, after a while your batteries will never fully recharge. Check the manual that came with your batteries. Most batteries work best if kept in a recharger when not in use.

Lenses

Clean your lenses with a lens cleaning solution and special tissues, both of which are available at your camera store. Do not use window cleaning spray liquids and tissues or paper towels. They will damage the lens coating.

PRODUCTION TECHNIQUES

Long Shot

Close-up

THE CAMERA
Shots

Students should practice looking through the camera viewfinder and visualizing the shots they want to make. A variety of shots are possible, from a full frontal shot, in which the camera is aimed directly at the front of the subject, to a sideways shot or an over-the-shoulder shot. Each of these shots can be further refined according to how close the camera is to the subject and whether the lens has zoomed in or out, from a full-length shot to a close-up. These refinements can be further divided into camera angle—whether the camera is looking down on the subject or looking up at the subject.

Students should keep in mind that each kind of shot conveys a subtle message to the audience. For example, an extreme close-up of a subject's face taken while the subject is talking would tend to heighten the dramatic quality of what the person is saying and focus on the person's internal qualities. Compare this shot with a full-length shot taken from below: the subject would appear distant and imposing.

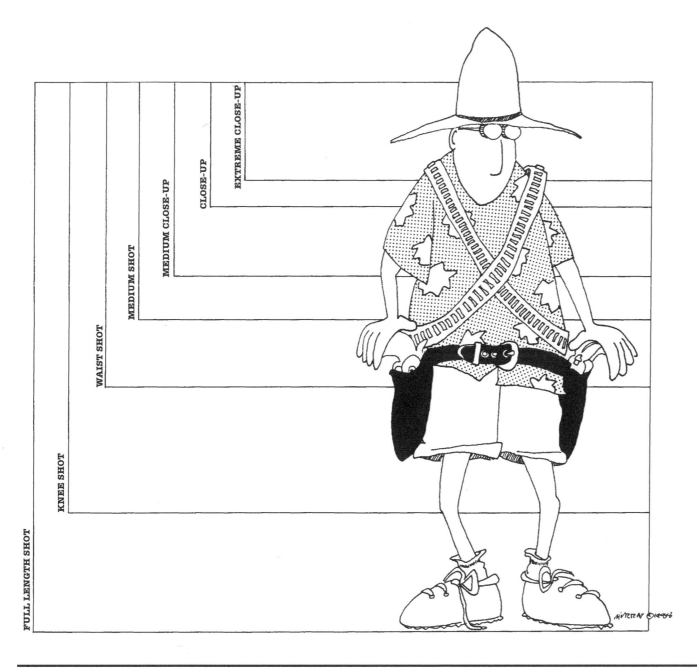

FULL LENGTH SHOT

KNEE SHOT

WAIST SHOT

MEDIUM SHOT

MEDIUM CLOSE-UP

CLOSE-UP

EXTREME CLOSE-UP

Choose your shots carefully, not only for their visual quality but also for the emotional impact they will have on the audience.

PRODUCTION TECHNIQUES

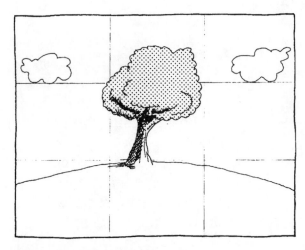

A   Less Visual Interest

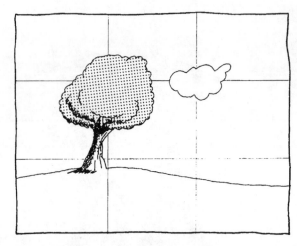

B   More Visual Interest

C   With Thirds

D   With Talking Space

Framing the Shot

Once students select the kind of shot they want—for example, medium close-up—ask the cameraperson to divide the frame mentally into thirds horizontally and vertically. The intersections of the lines are where the viewer tends to focus. With this focus in mind, give them these few hints to greatly improve their videos:

- Avoid the center of the frame (see illustration A, left); place the subject at one of the intersections for more visual interest (illustration B).
- Keep the speaker's eyes about two-thirds from the bottom of the frame (illustration C).
- Avoid cutting off subjects' heads when taping a group of people.

PRODUCTION TECHNIQUES

Dolly

Pan

Truck

Tilt

- Give the subject "talking space" or "looking room" (illustration D) on the screen—allow for extra space on the side toward which the subject is talking or looking. Failure to balance a shot in this way is a common error among novices.

When framing a shot, students should pay attention to how something looks through the viewfinder, not just how it looks in real life. They need to make sure the scene in the viewfinder is balanced. Encourage them to balance for color as well, remembering that bright colors draw attention and busy backgrounds (those with a lot of detail or action) tend to overwhelm a subject. To change color imbalance, they will change the lighting or move the subject or camera for a new angle, lighting, or emphasis.

Movement

Once students begin taping, they will want to change the picture in the frame. A full minute of a single shot can be boring indeed! Several camera moves are possible:

Zoom: When the camera lens zooms in or out, it actually changes the focal length of the lens or the distance between the lens and the recording surface without moving the camera. Zooming in gives the appearance of moving in on the subject. Zooming out gives the appearance of moving out. To zoom in or out, the cameraperson smoothly presses the zoom toggle button on the camera—the *T* side of the button (for *telephoto*) zooms in and the *W* side (for *wide angle*) zooms out. I tell students that if they have trouble remembering that *T* is for *telephoto* and *W* is for *wide angle*, they should remember that *T* is for *Toward* the subject and *W* is for *a-Way* from the subject. Many amateurs make the mistake of zooming in when they want to zoom out and vice versa.

PRODUCTION TECHNIQUES

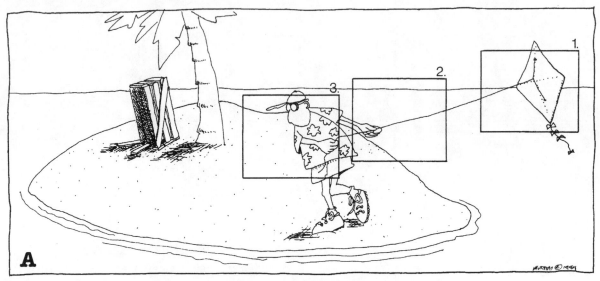

Dolly in or out: Used as a verb, *dolly* means to move the whole camera toward or away from the subject. The cameraperson can do so most smoothly when the camera is mounted on a steady object such as a tripod or dolly.

Pan: The cameraperson pivots the camera from side to side. Most people tend to pan without first deciding where they are panning!

Truck: The cameraperson moves the camera left or right to follow the subject.

Pan as transition

Tilt: The cameraperson pivots the camera to point up or down, with one side higher than the other.

Each movement produces certain effects. Normally, for example, the cameraperson should pan slowly and smoothly so the video audience can follow the camera shot easily. Panning quickly so that the background becomes a blur, however, may help change from one scene to another. Each movement has its own challenges, so be sure students practice!

One final note: Always point the camera lens away from the lights or the sun! Direct light can permanently damage the lens.

Transitions

Many basic camera moves may also serve as transitions from one scene to another. As the subject moves, for example, students can pan or tilt to follow the action. To conclude a scene, they might want to zoom in on the subject's face or zoom out to a full-length shot of the subject standing. Transitions are done smoothly and well only with a lot of practice.

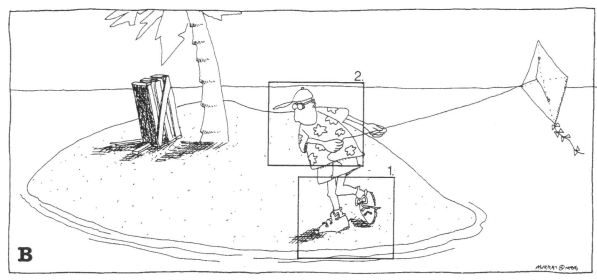

Tilt as transition

Zoom as transition

Two other transitions are also available:

- To *iris down* means to gradually close the iris of the lens to create a fade. Note that the cameraperson must iris down manually.
- Students can quickly put black cardboard in front of the lens. They must do it quickly or it will look silly.

Transitions

A. Pan as transition
   Frame 1 to frame 3, pan left
   Frame 3 to frame 1, pan right
B. Tilt as transition
   Frame 1 to frame 2, tilt up
   Frame 2 to frame 1, tilt down
C. Zoom as transition (note there is always some panning when you zoom)
   Frame 1 to frame 2, zoom out
   Frame 2 to frame 1, zoom in

CHOICE OF VIDEO TREATMENT

Four basic types of video treatment are described at the right. There are more than these basic types, of course, and some video productions may combine types. When helping students plan a treatment for their video production, keep in mind that some subjects suggest certain treatments. A video production about the effects of divorce on children, for example, would be particularly dramatic, whereas a video production of a student council meeting would probably be simple documentary. By mixing treatments, however, or using a treatment seemingly unsuitable for the subject, students may produce interesting, creative results.

Note that the video productions described in "Video Production in 9 Easy Lessons" are *studio productions*, that is, students prepare a script and storyboard and other students act out parts in a controlled setting. An alternative to studio video is *process video*, videotaping

Educational videos demonstrate how something works, present factual information, or describe something.

Humorous videos are meant to make people laugh.

Documentary videos record for historical purposes some event or occurrence.

Dramatic videos are meant to dramatize some fictional or nonfictional story.

that records live, unrehearsed action. The uses for process video are myriad: to record artistic or athletic performances, to provide feedback for artistic or athletic training, or to monitor progress in a learning situation. Studio production is easier for beginning students because the setting is more controlled and basic video techniques play a greater role, but process video can be an important aspect of video production as well. An optional lesson plan on process videos is provided in the appendix on page 98.

LIGHTING

Students can light a set with only one light—called the *key spot*—usually above the camera and off to one side. They can light a set with two lights: the key spot on one side and a smaller light—the *fill light*—off to the other side. Three lights give even better lighting: the key

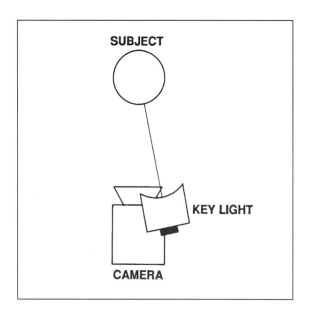

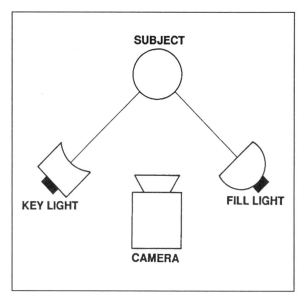

spot and the fill light as described above and a third light—the back light—behind the subject.

Students can achieve special effects with lighting from various angles—above, below, behind, to the side. They can also use colored filters for effect, but they should use them carefully. Lights get hot!

If lights are too harsh, consider recommending students use a reflector or bounce light off a white ceiling to diffuse the glare. Observe safety precautions at all times.

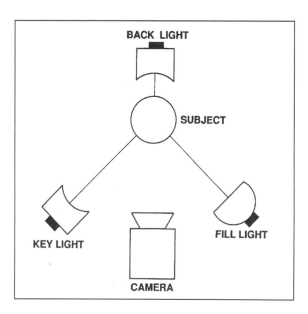

Remember, lighting is an art, a whole field in itself, so keep things simple at first until students get more experience. There is plenty of room to grow!

WHITE BALANCING

Your eyes and brain adjust automatically to changes in the color of light. A videocamera is not that flexible. Most cameras come with a daylight/indoor light switch, also called a *white balancing switch*. White balancing tells the camera what *white* is—the camera adjusts for the other colors from there. Some newer cameras come with an automatic white balancing feature, which can be very convenient. If a camera does not white balance automatically, students must place something white—a shirt, poster, or piece of paper—in the lighting they will be using and press the white balance switch. They must fill the frame with the white object—zoom in so only the white source shows—and turn on all sources of light. This process will fine-tune the camera.

If everything in a taped scene is off color, they probably forgot to adjust the white balance.

Remind them to readjust the camera every time they move to different lighting!

SOUND

Student videographers usually obtain adequate sound from the microphone built into the camera. Be aware, however, that the built-in microphone will pick up sound from everywhere, including the cameraperson. Furthermore, the voice of and sounds made by the cameraperson may be recorded more loudly than any other sound because he or she is closest to the microphone! Also beware of fluorescent lights—they hum! Your students can usually reduce or eliminate these problems by using additional or external microphones.

Although the built-in microphone is usually sufficient, at certain times students may need additional microphones, such as for an interview or when recording in a large room.

Sound or audio techniques can be complex—which is why many professionals make a living doing sound—but the techniques need not be overwhelming. If students want to use additional microphones in their video production, ask your school's theater or music instructor for help, contact your local music store for suggestions, or check your local library or the internet for additional references.

If students want to add sound to their completed videotape or change the sound they have, they will need to undertake some *audio dubbing*, which I explain further on page 31.

GRAPHICS

Graphics is the term generally applied to the signs or written material used in a video production—the title, credits, and so forth. If your students want graphics to appear in their finished videotapes, they will need to create them to record on camera. Every student seems to enjoy creating graphics.

One word of caution: Since they will be aiming the camera at the graphic and then recording it, the display must fill the frame completely. They do not want to record the wood chair supporting the posterboard in their attempt to squeeze in all the credit lines! Students must leave a border around the edge of the posterboard. Three or four inches all the way around should suffice. Encourage them to use the center of the posterboard for their graphic, remembering that a television screen is proportioned on a 4-to-3 ratio: four units across by three units down. A television screen is not square. If students keep forgetting to leave a margin, cut a border to fit over the posterboard and ask them to trace it on the board before they begin.

What materials to use? Students can try butcher paper, posterboard, magnetic letters on the blackboard, letters on a feltboard, flying letters (letters suspended with fishline), press-type, computer-generated graphics, and so on. They will also need plenty of markers, glue, scissors, and erasers.

What graphics to include? Students might consider preparing a title for their video production, credits, transitions (such as "two days later" or "meanwhile"), and, of course, "The End"!

PRODUCTION CUES AND GESTURES

Many cues and gestures are used in video productions. Some are related to technical actions and expectations that amateur student crews need not know. Other basic gestures can simplify production work, however, and give a sense of professionalism to the production crew. Some of the basic gestures are illustrated at right. They are further explained in lesson 3 (pages 49–51).

5-4-3-2-1   STAND BY   SPEED UP   READY

CUT   STRETCH   ACTION   OK

EDITING

Editing is the arranging of taped scenes or "takes" into a finished form. There are two types of editing: in-camera editing and machine-to-machine editing.

In-Camera Editing

In-camera editing simply means to tape the scenes in the order in which they will appear in the final video. Students can tape several takes of one scene, but each time they retape a take, they will need to rewind the tape to the beginning of the previous take, and the previous take will be erased.

If students decide to tape only one take of each scene, they simply tape their beginning graphics, then pause or stop the camera and prepare the first scene. They tape the first scene, then pause or stop the camera and prepare the second scene, then tape the second scene, and so on until the video is finished. No further editing is required.

Machine-to-Machine Editing

Machine-to-machine editing allows for essentially reassembling the finished tape in any order one chooses. Students can tape the scenes in the order that is the easiest and put the takes together later in the proper sequence. They can save several takes of a single scene and choose the best one during editing.

Machine-to-machine editing can be done with two VCRs or, better yet, professional editing equipment. Portable editors are also available that do a passable edit. Your local video dealer can provide more information.

Before students start editing, they must log the tape, that is, review it slowly and take note of each scene and the counter numbers at which each scene disappears. I discuss this process in detail in lesson 8 (pages 69–70). A blank Edit Log form is included in the appendix on page 86.

Once students have logged the tape and chosen the scenes they want to appear in the finished video, they are ready to begin editing. If they are using two VCRs, they can machine-to-machine edit in two ways, depending on the kind of VCR they have, so be sure they check their manual.

PRODUCTION TECHNIQUES

Hook-up. One VCR will be the "player" and one will be the "recorder." Students will need a monitor for each. They will also need two separate cables with the correct plugs or a double Y cable with separate plugs. (These plugs are available at your local electronics store.) One cable connects the player VCR audio "out" with the recorder VCR audio "in," and one cable connects the video "out" on the player VCR to the video "in" on the recorder VCR. See the VCR manual for more specific instructions.

Timing. An important thing to remember is that both VCRs need about 3 to 5 seconds to get their tapes rolling at proper recording speed, that is, up to 5 seconds of stable video signal before students can begin editing. Failure to get up to speed results in "rainbows" or other distortions on the tape for the first few seconds. Outline both of the following procedures for students; they allow for 5 seconds of rolling time to get up to speed before the taping starts.

Procedure 1
- Insert a blank tape in the recorder VCR and a logged tape in the player VCR.
- Find the spot on the blank tape where you wish to begin (or resume) taping. Using your logging notes, find the scene on your logged tape that you wish to record. Record for about 30 seconds at the beginning so there is some blank tape.
- Set the counters to zero on both machines. Rewind both tapes about 5 counter numbers.

- Press "play" on both machines, then hit the "pause" buttons when the counters are two digits from zero. Press "play" on both machines again simultaneously.
- When the counters reach zero, hit the "record" button on the recorder VCR and let both machines roll until the end of the scene. Stop the machines, recue them, and begin the process again.

Procedure 2
- Insert a blank tape in the recorder VCR and the logged tape in the player VCR.
- Find the spot on the blank tape where you wish to begin (or resume) taping. Using your logging notes, find the scene on your logged tape that you wish to record.
- Set the counters to zero on both machines.

PRODUCTION TECHNIQUES

- Press the "record" button on the recorder VCR, then the "pause" button. Rewind the logged tape on the player VCR about 10 counter numbers, then hit the "play" button.
- When the beginning of the scene appears, take the recorder VCR out of pause to begin the recording. (Read your manual on this procedure for specific directions, however, because machines vary.)
- Let both machines roll until the end of the scene. Stop the machines, recue them, and begin the process again.

Students must practice, practice, practice! The only way to become adept at smooth, clean transitions between scenes is to practice. One nice thing about machine-to-machine editing, however, is that if they make a mistake, they can simply do it over!

AUDIO DUBBING

The type of VCR students have will determine if they can add sound or change sound on their tapes. Review the manual for directions. One word of advice: if they are going to play with audio dubbing, encourage them to make copies of their tapes and experiment with the copy to avoid erasing the audio on the original tape!

Stereo Sound. If the VCR is a stereo VCR, students can put additional sound on one electronic track and leave the original sound on the other track (for example, to add background music to an ocean shore scene). A stereo VCR should have two audio inputs for left- and right-hand channels. If it has only one input, the video dealer should have an adapter.

Sound-on-Sound. This feature allows students to add additional sound to the existing sound on a tape. See the VCR manual for directions.

Audio Dubbing. On some VCRs, adding additional sound to a tape means erasing the original sound. Newer VCRs have a special feature called *audio dub* that allows for adding sound without losing the original sound. See the VCR manual for directions.

VIDEO CREW

A video crew can consist of many people, but at least four positions are critical: producer, director, cameraperson, and "talent." Light and sound technicians may also be valuable, as well as a video technician. Each position has specific duties during the preproduction phase of the project, during production, and during postproduction. These duties are outlined at right.

Producer (The Boss!)
Preproduction
- makes the final decision regarding content, audience, and objectives of the production
- chooses and assigns responsibility to the director and lets the director choose, but has final say over, the scriptwriters, storyboard artists, crew members, and talent

Production
- oversees production but is not involved in the day-to-day responsibility unless he or she desires or is asked

Postproduction
- participates in logging and editing the tapes
- evaluates the artistic and technical quality of the production

Director
Preproduction
- is responsible for preparing the script and storyboard (although he or she may assign someone else to complete them)
- is responsible for the preparation of prop and equipment lists and the diagram of the set
- trains crew members for their various jobs
- calls for walk-throughs and rehearsals

Production
- calls the camera shots
- cues the talent and crew
- interprets the script and storyboard for the talent and crew

Postproduction
- participates in logging and editing the tapes
- evaluates the artistic and technical quality of the production

PRODUCTION TECHNIQUES

Cameraperson
Preproduction
- makes sure the crew members know their duties
- makes sure the crew members do their jobs
- helps prepare the set and props
- is familiar with the script and storyboard

Production
- operates the camera following the director's commands

Postproduction
- helps the director evaluate the production
- supervises the crew in disconnecting equipment and putting everything away

Talent
Preproduction
- helps crew members as needed
- memorizes the script and storyboard
- is ready for walk-throughs and rehearsals

Production
- follows the director's cues
- thinks about his or her part and characterization

Postproduction
- helps evaluate the production
- helps put away the equipment

Light and Sound Technician
Preproduction
- arranges for lighting and sound following the director's wishes

Production
- provides adequate light and sound during taping following director and cameraperson's commands
- helps set up and put away equipment

Video Technician
Production
- runs VCR if separate from camera
- provides appropriate cues (such as "tape rolling")
- helps set up and put away equipment

PRODUCTION TECHNIQUES

Other crew positions may be necessary depending on the size of the production. These include a prop or set person, a costume and makeup person, and a graphics person. You can create positions as needed!

SPECIAL EFFECTS

Special effects expand the creativity of video production. Your students will be fascinated with them, so allow lots of time for them to experiment.

The viewer's mind actually creates the effect, so students don't need to be elaborate. They should keep shots short and effects simple. Simple effects work best when they are scripted ahead of time.

Ask students to shoot tight (close up). Wide shots are not effective, especially with low budget effects.

Don't leave a shot on screen long enough for the viewer to figure out how it was done. And don't overdo; too many effects will bore the audience.

Remind students to include audio effects. Sound is as important as video in making an effect clear and powerful.

Here's some simple effects and how tos:

Animation

Students can use clear thread or fishing line, lighting, or special backgrounds to make objects move. They can also stop and start the camera ("stop action") and move objects between takes. This method may require some editing.

Each camera has its own *roll time*. To determine the roll time of your camera, begin videotaping a clock as the second hand hits 12. Press stop when it comes to 12 again. On playback, you'll be able to see how long it takes the images to appear on your video.

Makeup

Flour (not talcum powder) creates surprisingly realistic gray hair. Eyeliner will draw great mustaches and beards. Baby oil makes someone appear sweaty during a chase scene. All kinds of makeup materials are available cheaply just after Halloween. Monitor your students carefully to make sure they are using the materials safely.

A word about blood: Many adolescents are fascinated with gore and want to create and focus on it during a scene. Discourage this fascination and challenge your students to focus (literally) on a story and not the effects.

PRODUCTION TECHNIQUES

Weather

Your camcorder will work best in moderate conditions. Cold weather will cause your lens to fog. Very hot weather can damage some electronic components in the camera. For obvious reasons, avoid being out in the rain, snow, or lightning storms. And of course, do not take a camera underwater! Students can use awnings, car interiors, or tents to protect the camera while filming something outdoors.

To create outdoor effects, however, there are a lot of things students can do. They can fill an aquarium with water, then use a baster to inject liquid tempera into the water, stirring it to simulate a raging storm. Injecting milk along the bottom of the aquarium will create a foglike effect. Be aware that the temperature of the water can change the effect. Students film through the side of the aquarium for both effects. Don't use oil-based paints!

Students can use a fan to simulate wind. They can also tie strings to bushes and trees and pull on them to simulate wind, especially if they want to avoid the noise a fan makes.

Fire

Pyrotechnics are much too dangerous for students to attempt. They can simulate smoke, however, by using a vaporizer.

Starry Night

My students got a great effect by poking holes in black bulletin-board paper and then backlighting it with a projector.

Lighting

Students can use the manual iris on the camera to create flashes of brilliant light or other bizarre effects. Just open the iris all the way quickly.

Models

Students can use a model or painted picture of an object or location to really add to the effects. Use camera angles and lighting to help. Using models is an effective way to film a car or plane crash.

PRODUCTION TECHNIQUES

Filters

Shooting through a vertical pane of glass with water running down it can give a really cool effect. Students can also use colored pantyhose as great substitutes for expensive filters. Different colors will produce dramatically different effects. Students can stretch the hose over the lens and experiment. Students might also tape lens cleaning paper over the lens to give a light, misty look to a shot. They'll need to set the lens at full telephoto so the texture isn't too obvious.

Other filter ideas include colanders, plastic wrap, aluminum or tin foil with holes punched in it, stained glass, kaleidoscopes, window screens, colored bottles, small leafed plants—ask students to experiment with these and others to see the effects!

Video Feedback

This effect is very psychedelic, great for music videos! Be sure to turn down the audio, or you'll have audio feedback as well! Aim your camera so it videotapes the TV screen of your monitor. Connect your camcorder to the monitor so you can see the camcorder's image on the TV. If you can generate characters with your camcorder, do it. Then try panning and tilting. The effect changes constantly, so experiment.

Gravity Effects

To simulate talent defying gravity, students simply change the position of the camera. They hold it sideways to tape someone climbing up a "wall," upside down (with the appropriate set) to tape someone on the "ceiling."

Mirrors

Students can use mirrors to avoid placing camcorders in dangerous situations (a pitcher throwing a ball at the camera, for example), or to create split-screen effects. They can also use mirrors to add lighting or images to a scene.

PRODUCTION TECHNIQUES

HINTS AND CAUTIONS

To prevent permanent damage to the camera, remind camerapeople to point the camera away from the sun or lights at all times. When the camera is not in use, keep the lens cap on.

Remind students to check all cable connections. Tape a trial scene and review it. One class lost a whole day's taping because the microphone cord was not properly attached, and no sound was recorded. (One way to avoid this particular mishap is to use headphones and monitor what is being recorded.)

Remind students to check all equipment for tight attachments. You would hate to lose a camera because of a loose screw or bolt.

Remind students to make all camera moves S-L-O-W-L-Y. Pan, tilt, and zoom carefully.

Special effects can get boring quickly. Caution students against overdoing them.

Remind students to white balance before they begin and every time the lighting changes.

Ask students to label all tapes (date, subject, approximate length of recording).

Remind students not to leave the camera in "pause" for too long. It will wear out the tape and dirty the VCR heads. If students will not be recording for a while, they should turn the camera to "stop."

Ask students to vary shots to add interest. They might tape each scene from different angles.

If students want to **save their tapes**, break out the "erase-protect" tabs (see the instructions that come with the tape).

VIDEO PRODUCTION IN 9 EASY LESSONS

Lesson 1 What Makes an Effective Production?

Lesson 2 The Mechanics: Simple Scripts and Storyboards

Lesson 3 Introducing Equipment: Producing a Simple Interview

Lesson 4 Selecting a Program Treatment

Lesson 5 Production: Technique, Terminology, Technicians

Lesson 6 Organizing for Video Production

Lesson 7 The Production!

Lesson 8 Logging and Editing Rough Footage

Lesson 9 Evaluation, Student-Style

LESSON 1
WHAT MAKES AN EFFECTIVE PRODUCTION?

TEACHER'S OBJECTIVES

- to review the elements of any production—theme, setting, plot, mood, characterizations
- to help students analyze a production for its elements
- to help students understand the importance of the relationships between production elements
- to help students construct a chart of criteria to use in evaluating productions

STUDENTS' OBJECTIVES

- to identify the elements of a video production
- to identify the effective qualities of a television show
- to analyze and evaluate a current high-quality television show

FUNDAMENTALS

Before students can begin to produce videos, they need to evaluate the qualities of *effective* video productions. Just about all students have seen effective video productions, but usually they have not analyzed them for the elements that make them effective. Students will need to pay attention to these elements to use them effectively.

One concept that is crucial to video production is *layering*. Layering is present in every effective production. It is the deliberate choice of elements that appeal to a variety of audiences. For example, *The Cosby Show*, a popular situation comedy in the 1980s, appeals to a variety of people because

- the characters represent several age groups
- politics and racism, even feminism, are brought up in the series, and each attracted its share of the audience
- the interactions of the characters are readily identifiable to a majority of the audience (we all argued the issues at home, too!)
- the characterizations, although stereotypical, are generic enough that each audience member can identify with a character's good points and bad ones (we are drawn to these contradictions—we find them humorous)
- the plots are realistic in the way problems arise and delightful in the creative and comic way in which problems are solved

Nevertheless, simply throwing together a variety of elements (such as certain distinct personalities) without thinking about their "fit" with the other characters, theme, setting, plot, or mood does not guarantee success. The point is, *it is the conscious use of related elements that appeal to various audiences simultaneously that makes a video effective.* It is the interplay among these elements that makes the magic work. All successful programs have layering.

Note that if you choose to show good layering techniques to your class, you will have to choose an age-appropriate show as your example. Many situation comedies or dramas may not be appropriate for your students.

STUDENTS WILL NEED TO KNOW

- theme, setting, plot, mood, and characterization as elements of any production
- ways to analyze a production for these elements
- popular classic or contemporary television shows

MATERIALS

- a preselected written work to analyze in class, such as a selection from Junior Great Books, Mother Goose poems, or a fable or myth such as "Snow White"
- a preselected, age-appropriate video recording of a current high-quality television show to analyze in class (be sure to follow copyright restrictions)

- a chalkboard and chalk or chart paper and markers
- a VCR and television to show the video recording

VOCABULARY*

Characterizations
Criteria
Mood
Plot
Setting
Theme

*Vocabulary words in each lesson are defined in the glossary, page 106.

PROCEDURES

Preparation: Ask students if they have ever created their own television show and ask if it was a lot of work. Tell them that making television shows can be a lot of fun if they understand the basics of producing shows. Tell them that by the end of the day's lesson they will understand what makes a good television show great.

1. **Brainstorm TV shows.** Ask students to think of the names of television shows, past and present. Record all responses on the chalkboard. Then ask students to name past and present "hit" shows, ones that they think were successful or popular. Add any that are not already there to the list on the board. Guide this compilation so that it includes classic shows (older shows generally recognized for high quality), especially those currently in syndication.

2. **Compare most and least favorite shows.** Ask students to name their favorite shows, either from the list or not. Write them on the chalkboard. Then ask students to name their least favorite programs and list these as well. Compare these two lists and discuss, using the following questions to begin the discussion:

Are any shows on both lists?

Why did you choose each particular show?

How have your choices changed as you have grown older?

What could account for the differences in choices?

3. **Recall the elements of a dramatic work.** Ask students to identify the elements of a book. They are theme, setting, plot, characterization, and mood. Ask them to define the elements and give examples of each. Select a television show from the previous lists and ask students to identify the dramatic elements in it.

4. **Ask students to identify the dramatic elements in the pre-selected written work.**

5. **Analyze the elements for effectiveness.** Ask students, "What makes a good plot?" Then, "What makes a good theme?" You will probably get answers like "those that are realistic, believable, original." Ask them to discuss the characteristics of effective elements, which will lead them to discover interrelationships among elements. Someone will probably say, "The setting must match the theme." Point out that to be effective, the elements must "fit" with one another in some way. Ask students to provide other examples.

6. **Construct a "Criteria for Evaluation" chart.** This chart will include observations and requirements noted by the students, for example, "Does the time setting match the theme?" Point out that, to be effective, the chart must be applicable to any video production with a script. (News, educational television, and documentaries are excluded.) Post this chart in a conspicuous location and refer to it frequently!

7. **Evaluate a favorite TV show using this chart.** Discuss the "hit" shows listed on the board for a few minutes by asking the students, "Why are these shows successful?" This serves to refresh students' memories about the shows and also to familiarize everyone with the basic concepts of the shows cited.

8. **Evaluate the tape of a TV show using this chart.** Let's hope that your recording will be of a tele-vision show on the students' list. Have the class watch a selection from the show, per-haps even an entire program, and then analyze the show for its elements using the Criteria for Evaluation.

9. **Homework activity.** Students choose a popular dramatic tele-vision program (not a game show or a documentary, but a sitcom, mystery, and so on) and analyze it for the basic story elements discussed thus far. They will write a review of it.

EXTENSION ACTIVITY

Students could create an outline of the basic story elements for an orig-inal dramatic television script. The outline should include a description of the main characters, a descrip-tion of the setting, a summary of the plot, a description of the mood, and a statement of the theme.

LESSON 2
THE MECHANICS: SIMPLE SCRIPTS AND STORYBOARDS

TEACHER'S OBJECTIVES
- to define the specialized terminology appropriate to video scripts and storyboards
- to help each student create a script and storyboard for a simple interview

STUDENT'S OBJECTIVES
- to identify basic production terminology and techniques
- to develop a simple script
- to develop a simple storyboard
- to use a variety of camera angles and shots in creating a script and storyboard

FUNDAMENTALS
Having analyzed the elements that contribute to effective video productions, students can now better understand production elements—what converts ideas into reality. A script and a storyboard help structure ideas into practical, cohesive concepts that have form and flow.

STUDENTS WILL NEED TO KNOW
- the meaning of the terms *audio* and *video*

MATERIALS
- overhead transparencies of the sample script and storyboard sheets (pages 81–82) and markers
- blank copies of the script and storyboard forms as work sheets (pages 84–85)
- optional: transparencies of video equipment, camera shots, and camera transitions (see "The Basics" and "Production Techniques")
- a demonstration set-up: camera, lights (if necessary), and, if possible, a monitor connected to the camera so students can see what the cameraperson sees

VOCABULARY
Close-up
Cut
Fade in/fade out
Long shot
Medium shot
Pan
Tilt
Zoom in/Zoom out

PROCEDURES

Preparation: Ask students if any of them have ever been on television or visited a television studio. Allow them to share their experiences for a moment, then tell them that by the end of the day's lesson, they will have planned their own short interview in which each class member will get to be on camera. (Ignore the groans now—they will really enjoy this!)

1. **Identify video equipment.** Ask students to list types of equipment used in a television studio. You might want to display overhead transparencies of "Basic Equipment" (pages 9–11) to fill in any gaps in their knowledge. Relate their list to the equipment you plan to use in your classroom. For example, if you will not be using separate microphones, point this out.

2. **Identify camera shots.** Next, use the camera and a transparency of "The Camera—Shots" (pages 18–20) and point out differences between shots. The demonstration is important: it is good practice for you, and it increases your credibility with students. If some students are proficient with a camera, ask them to demonstrate some shots. If they have not yet used a video camera, go easy on the demonstrations until later.

   For practice, ask students to identify the various camera shots used in a specific short video sequence such as a commercial, an introduction to a television show, or a news commentary.

3. **Identify camera transitions.**
Display a transparency of "The Camera—Movement" (page 21) and "The Camera—Transitions" (page 22), and discuss transitions. Demonstrate each transition, being sure that students know what knobs, buttons, or levers produce each effect when using your equipment. Remember, you are not only teaching terminology, you are also familiarizing students with the equipment so they can produce a video. Ask students to demonstrate each of these moves.

4. **Identify part of a script.** Tell students that today they will be creating their own scripts and storyboards for a real video. Display a transparency (or distribute copies) of the sample script (page 81). Ask students to note that the script is divided into two sections—"Audio" and "Video."

5. **Define the purposes of the audio and video sections of a script.**
Using the sample script, ask students to note that the audio section of the script details the spoken or audio section of the production. Words to be spoken are written in capital and lowercase letters. The video portion contains directions for the cameraperson, director, and other crewmembers. These directions are always written in capital letters. Point out the terminology used and indicate that, in creating a script, the writer must anticipate the visual shot needed for each section.

6. **Identify parts of a storyboard.**
Display a transparency (or distribute copies) of the sample storyboard (page 82) from the same sample production as the sample script. Ask students to differentiate between the script and the storyboard. Note that the purpose of a storyboard is not to be artistic but to give a visual impression of each scene. Also note that camera transitions are identified between the scenes of the storyboard to clarify how the cameraperson moves from one shot to another. As practice, you might want to create a simple storyboard together in class, using an overhead transparency storyboard form.

7. **Create a simple script.** Divide the class into groups of three or four students (or let the students choose their own groups). These groups will be working together for a while, so be sure they can work together! Now direct each group to create its own short interview with the following structure: a host or hostess greets the television audience, introduces the guest and identifies the guest's purpose for appearing, asks the guest one simple question that the guest answers, then thanks the guest for appearing and the television audience for watching. Each group should use a blank script sheet (page 84). The students may be as creative as they can in naming the show, the host or hostess, and the guest, and in writing the conversation. (For the moment, encourage students to contain their creativity to the audio portion of the script.)

Ask the groups to write out their planned interview, taking care to draw lines between any sections of dialogue that are separated by camera cuts. Remind them of the use of capital and lowercase letters for the audio section of the script and all capitals for the video section.

8. **Create a simple storyboard.** As soon as each group agrees on the basics of the script, start some members of each group on their storyboard. The storyboard should illustrate the script that each group is writing.

Remember: Each group is writing only one script and storyboard. In the next lesson, each member of the group will rotate in the jobs of host or hostess, guest, cameraperson, and director for his or her group's script.

You may want to collect the groups' scripts and storyboards and make copies for each member, or they can make their own copies. When each group has completed its script and storyboard, members may spend extra time blocking their script, that is, rehearsing the script as if they were actually recording it. They could even create backdrops or costumes. This process is fine and fun, but do not let the embellishments take away from the real purpose: constructing effective scripts and storyboards.

Remind the groups that each member will get to act each part and will be taped doing it!

Next comes the FUN PART!

LESSON 3
INTRODUCING EQUIPMENT: PRODUCING A SIMPLE INTERVIEW

TEACHER'S OBJECTIVES

- to assist students in the production of a short video interview
- to encourage students to use a variety of camera angles and shots in their camerawork
- to demonstrate the use of correct directing terminology and gestures
- to demonstrate correct framing techniques

STUDENTS' OBJECTIVES

- to define the roles of the video production personnel
- to use a script, storyboard, and production techniques effectively to complete a video interview
- to use a video camera competently
- to use simple directing techniques effectively

FUNDAMENTALS

Students will apply what they have learned in the two previous lessons to produce an effective video interview. The main purpose of this lesson is to familiarize students with the video camera—being both in front of and behind it—and to use correct directing techniques.

THE TEACHER WILL NEED TO KNOW

- how to use the camera to achieve a close-up, medium, and long shot; to fade in, fade out, zoom in, zoom out, cut, pan, and tilt
- basic lighting; a simple lighting set-up will suffice (see "Lighting," page 25)
- how to record with the camera and play back the tape on a monitor using the camcorder or a VCR
- simple camera framing techniques (see "The Camera— Framing the Shot," page 20)
- the duties of the director, the cameraperson, and talent (see "Video Crew," page 32). It is especially important to stress the hierarchy of responsibility within the video crew. If you strictly enforce that the sole job of the cameraperson is to operate the camera under the direction of the director, and something goes wrong, then the culprit will be obvious. Remember, the director is headquarters. He or she tells everyone what to do, and if the talent or the cameraperson does not like it—well, that person can be director next time!

STUDENTS WILL NEED TO KNOW

- how to read a script and storyboard
- how to use the camera in a simple fashion

MATERIALS

- a set-up for taping the interviews (a camera with a VCR or camcorder, tripod, and so forth; see pages 9–11).
- simple lighting (see page 25).
- simple background: a desk and two chairs for the interview is fine
- videotapes—one should do

- a monitor: having a monitor rigged to a VCR (if you are using a separate camera and VCR) or to the camcorder is exceedingly helpful. Not only can the director see what the cameraperson sees, but the entire class will watch avidly so that they can do better when it's their turn!
- yarn and masking tape
- sample photographs. You may want to have posters or pictures of famous photographs for the students to analyze when discussing composition.

VOCABULARY

Cut
Ready cue
Roll tape
Stand by
Tape rolling
Time cues (5, 4, 3, 2, 1)
You're on (action)

PROCEDURES

Preparation: Remind students that each person will get the chance to be the host or hostess, guest, cameraperson, and director. Each team will rotate jobs until every member has had a turn in each job. At the end of the lesson, all teams will view the tape and critique each video for both good and bad points. Also, tell students that they will be learning a simple "trick" to make their video and even their photographs more interesting!

If a team has only three members, you can rotate into the fourth position or ask for a student volunteer. Having the teacher on the crew can provide a more mature example of proper behavior and technique.

Be sure to be lavish in your praise of good points and keep any negative comments brief, infrequent, and constructive. Encourage students to do the same. See page 79 for some positive comments you can use.

1. **Locate effective framing points.** Basic camera shot composition is important. Using the camera and monitor, ask a "victim" to sit on the set, then divide the screen into thirds horizontally and vertically by taping yarn across the monitor.

Tell the class that the basic idea is to place the main elements on the screen at one of the four intersections. Also point out that the eyes of a person on the screen are usually placed on an imaginary line two-thirds of the way up from the bottom of the screen. Demonstrate by using the camera and monitor.

Display some famous photographs and analyze their composition. If none is available, ask students to bring in examples of well-composed photographs and to watch for effective composition as they watch television.

2. **Define the roles of director, cameraperson, and talent.** Discuss with the class the various roles they will be undertaking. Point out that the job of the talent (the host or hostess and guest) is to interpret the role, but only with the approval of the director. The cameraperson also does only what the director says. If the director forgets to say "cut!" then the cameraperson does not cut. It is much easier later on if these roles are clear from the beginning. Remind students: This is not a democratic project!

3. **Demonstrate effective directing techniques.** Walk the students through a sample interview with you as director. The sequence should go as follows:

- Once the talent is in place and the cameraperson is ready, the director shouts, "Stand by!" only to inform the people nearby that taping is imminent. Upon hearing this, all audible talking and noise should stop. Do not let students use this phrase at other times simply to get quiet!

- The director, holding his or her hand in a "ready" cue, looks around the room to determine the readiness of the group. The director then turns to the cameraperson and says, "Roll tape."

- The cameraperson starts recording and checks to see that the tape is rolling by watching the VCR counters or light in the camera monitor. (Another person can do this at the VCR if it is separate.) The cameraperson (or person at the VCR) responds, "Tape rolling." Be sure the tape is rolling!

- The director places a hand where the talent will be looking when the scene begins (for example, next to the camera lens if the talent is looking directly at the camera) and gestures 5, 4, 3, 2, 1 while simultaneously calling out "5, 4, 3 . . ." The director does not call "2, 1." Allowing five seconds of "roll time" at the beginning and end of each scene is necessary for editing later on. **NEVER SKIP THIS STEP!**

- When the director points at or cues the talent in some other way, the talent begins the scene and continues until the end of the scene. At the end of the scene, the talent freezes and the director gestures 5, 4, 3, 2, 1 while simultaneously calling " . . . 3, 2, 1, CUT!" Note that the director does not call "5, 4 . . ." **NEVER SKIP THIS STEP!** Do not allow students to play around with these steps. You will see how drastically important they are when you edit, believe me.

4. **Videotape.** Now we're ready! Select a group to begin and instruct the other groups to watch. You may want to act as director the first time. Ask students to select their roles. Quickly review with the cameraperson the various switches and buttons that he or she will need to know. While the cameraperson experiments with the camera, instruct the talent to review the script. If you are not the director, review the director's steps with the person in that role.

Make sure everything is ready (lights? sound? VCR? tape?) and GO!

After the first round with this brave group, stop, rewind the tape, and view it. Check for sound levels, lighting, and so forth. The group will die of embarrassment. Smile! Now a new group takes its turn.

Tape all the groups, making sure every student has a chance at every role. Do not allow anyone to back out of a part. Tell them they must do this simple experiment now to understand what they will do later. Tell them they can choose the role they would like in subsequent lessons. For now, they need to try all the roles.

5. **Evaluate.** At the end of the session, view the tape from the entire session. Do not take the yarn off the monitor. Let students see for themselves that what they see in the camera viewfinder is not necessarily what happens on the screen. Again, be lavish in your positive feedback and easy on the criticism. Students will be self-critical enough without your help. Remind them that this lesson is only the beginning and the object of it is to learn to use the video equipment. Tell them you did not expect perfection (this time). Smile!

LESSON 4
SELECTING A PROGRAM TREATMENT

TEACHER'S OBJECTIVES

- to help students select a video treatment for their original production
- to help students generate ideas for their video production

STUDENTS' OBJECTIVES

- to differentiate among types of program treatments
- to select a program treatment for the video production
- to participate in the initial planning for a video production

FUNDAMENTALS

Now students can begin work on their own video productions. Allow them to work as a class or in small, self-selected groups. Deciding which way to go usually requires a class discussion, and the groups may not be ready to choose right away. Some students may want to see what the whole class is doing before they decide whether they want to do their own production. Allow them time to decide, but establish a firm deadline after which students cannot switch.

Regarding the size of each team, only you know your class well enough to structure the sizes. I have found that when my entire class works on a single project, things are much simpler, but I have also had excellent results with small groups within a class. For your sanity, try to limit the number of groups within a classroom to four.

Soon students will begin to meet in their production teams to discuss choices and arrange duties. The first big decision each team will make is the kind of video to do.

THE TEACHER WILL NEED TO KNOW

- the differences between the various types of program treatments: documentary, humorous, dramatic, educational, or combinations of these (see "Choice of Video Treatment," page 24)
- the steps each production team must go through to produce a finished video. The students will be developing a Video Production Proposal (pages 96–97) that will structure their thoughts and enthusiasm, but you will need to focus their energies in specific directions at certain times. At this point the primary focus should be on the completion of the Video Production Proposal.

Once students complete each section of the proposal, the team will have a more specific direction for their production.

Keep in mind at this early stage that students must choose the kind of editing they will do before they begin:

in-camera editing, which requires that students record the scenes (and graphics) in the order in which they will appear OR
machine-to-machine editing, which allows students to record several takes of each scene in nonsequential order and later reassemble the tape into finished form OR
computer (nonlinear) editing, which is an excellent way to edit video

In-camera editing requires careful planning and coordination during recording but no further editing after the taping is finished. You have your finished product! Machine-to-machine editing gives you greater flexibility during recording, but it requires a lot of editing time later. Computer editing is possible if your classroom computer has a video input/output card and you have access to appropriate video editing software. Learning to use the software can be time consuming, but the ultimate reward can be a great tape and access to superb effects! Follow the directions in your software manual.

STUDENTS WILL NEED TO KNOW

- camera shots and transitions discussed in the last lesson
- the basic purpose of a script and storyboard

MATERIALS

- copies of the Video Production Proposal (pages 96–97)
- optional: videotapes of previous student productions
- optional: a transparency of "Choice of Video Treatment" (page 24)

VOCABULARY

Types of Treatments
Dramatic
Documentary
Educational
Humorous

PROCEDURES

Preparation: Tell students that this is the day on which they will begin planning their own original video production. If you have a special goal for this video (for example, to show it at an open house or to enter it in a contest), explain that goal now. Give the class a rough sense of the schedule (for example, "We have three weeks in which to plan, tape, and complete this video. Planning will take at least one week, . . ."). Tell students that they can decide how to work on this video—whether in teams or as an entire class—but first you need to describe the kinds of videos they can produce.

1. **Differentiate among types of program treatments.** You may want to display a transparency of "Choice of Video Treatment" (page 24). Review and discuss the various types of program treatments: educational, dramatic, humorous, and documentary. Ask students to provide examples of each of these and to think of examples of programs that combine treatments. Point out that a video project does not have to be dramatic or have a story line. One class I taught did a wonderful job of videotaping interviews with kindergarten students to show incoming kindergartners, along with a companion video interviewing school personnel to show to the parents of the incoming students. Point out that often videos take an *old* subject or story line and give it a new *twist*—a new theme, characters, mood, or setting.

2. **Begin planning the video production.** Ask students to discuss how they would like to group themselves for this project. The discussion may take some time, or the class may be quite single minded. Try to hear all points of view. Guide the discussion if necessary to avoid personal comments. This discussion should reflect the goals and desires of students. After twenty minutes, end the discussion by pointing out that the final decision does not have to be reached yet. Tell students they can use some time to mull over their ideas. Announce that the final decision must be reached by the time production proposals are submitted, however, and give that date.

Now as a class, brainstorm the embryonic ideas the students have for videos. Place all these ideas on the blackboard and keep them there until the next class. Do not discuss any idea in detail. Praise students' participation. In your discussion, combine ideas or give them new twists. (In one of my classes, my students, who knew I was a member of an acting company that staged "murder weekends," were tickled when I suggested combining their idea of a kiddie video on dolls with a murder mystery. This idea developed into a wonderful murder mystery in which the dolls made their owners disappear.) Keep your comments light, supportive, and positive.

3. **Structure the production process.** Drawing an analogy to an iceberg; point out to the class that planning takes the most amount of time in any good production. Although the final production may last fifteen minutes, many hours will be, and must be, spent in planning. Such planning is the purpose of the Video Production Proposal: it forces students to plan. Planning, during which students will decide on their video's purpose, audience, elements, point of view, and format, will lead directly to design, during which students will develop script, storyboard, budget, and special needs such as props or costumes. Once the design is completed, production can begin.

After production, evaluation will complete the process.

4. **Introduce the video production proposal.** Distribute copies of the Video Production Proposal form and go over each step. Tell students that before they can begin designing, the Video Production Proposal must be approved by the executive producer—you!

Sometimes students get obsessed with violence and simple solutions to problems in their scripts. Invariably, videos in this format end up being superficial and boring. Be firm with these students in your demand for more thought and depth in their scripts. The proposal phase is a good time to share videos from previous classes or other groups of students and analyze them based on the criteria of effective videos your class developed in lesson 1. I have tried letting students produce superficial videos

(although I toned down the violence), and I found that letting them "fall on their faces" is not educationally effective here. They did not learn to change their scripts. It is effective to show these superficial videos to other classes, however, for evaluation. Students readily see the lack of quality. Include in the discussion of these sample videos reviews or critical comments from previous years as well, if you have them.

Now let students go to work on their Video Production Proposals!

LESSON 5
PRODUCTION: TECHNIQUE, TERMINOLOGY, TECHNICIANS

TEACHER'S OBJECTIVES
- to help students complete a script and storyboard for their video project
- to define the roles of the members of the production crew

STUDENTS' OBJECTIVES
- to define the basic roles of the production crewmembers
- to choose a format, purpose, audience, materials, and budget for their video project as outlined on the Video Production Proposal
- to participate effectively on a planning team for a video production

FUNDAMENTALS
You have started students in the production of their first video. Congratulations! Things may seem embryonic right now, but that's all right! You are at the mess stage in creative production. Soon vague hunches will begin to solidify into workable ideas. Be patient!

In this lesson students select a format for their video, complete their production proposal, begin writing their script and storyboard, choose crewmembers, and assign duties. They will make great strides toward the final realization of their production.

During this time students are making major decisions about what they want to do for their video. These decisions are still flexible and may change as teams revise their perception of what they can and cannot practically do. With the exception of the producer and director, crewmembers can change roles right through the taping. The producer—remember, you are the executive producer!—is the final authority. He or she retains the right to "fire" or "hire" the director and crewmembers. Encourage your producer to keep these power plays to a minimum.

The director is charged with getting the concept of the video on tape. He or she makes the script come to life, with real talent and real scenery. Because it is reality, however, the director's concept and the producer's concept may not match. It is your job to make sure that the producers and directors understand this fact and deal with it constructively.

THE TEACHER WILL NEED TO KNOW

- the responsibilities of each crewmember and the pecking order (see "Video Crew," page 32)
- how to produce effective graphics (see "Graphics," page 27)

STUDENTS WILL NEED TO KNOW

- how to create a script and storyboard
- how to develop a Video Production Proposal

MATERIALS

- copies of "Video Crew"

VOCABULARY

Audience
Director
Point of view
Producer
Talent
Teamwork

PROCEDURES

Preparation: Ask the class how they have decided to work. All groups should be solidified enough so that today they can choose their crewmembers and begin working in earnest. If a group is not this far, you may need to step in as executive producer and make some decisions for them. By the end of today's class, each group will have a producer and possibly a director. The main goal for this class time is to complete the Video Production Proposal.

1. **Define the basic roles of the video crew.** Distribute copies of "Video Crew." Review the duties of each technician and make sure that students understand not only what each technician does, but who has responsibility for what. Inform the class that you will support the following chain of command: if the cameraperson has a problem, he or she should go to the director first, then to the producer, and only then to the executive producer (you). The students will test this structure in the beginning, but if you stick to your word, they will learn to work out their differences among themselves, as they should.

2. **Choose a producer.** Ask each group to choose a producer and notify you of their choice. This person will answer to you. Make sure the group and the producer understand their responsibilities.

Can the producer be in the video? Yes, although I discourage it initially. I have found it works better if the producer stays detached. There are plenty of other jobs—graphics, costumes, props, even directing—that he or she can do during production. Can the director be in the video? Again, say no initially, but if during production you discover you need the director in the video, allow it.

Other crewmembers can be in the video when they are not needed for their jobs. Producers, directors, and others can be in another group's video if desired, but another group's video cannot conflict with their video. The home team comes first!

3. **Choose a director.** Ask each group's producer to choose a director. This choice is the group's first experience with the hierarchy. If you have convinced them of the need for a definite structure, you will have no problems here. Allow large groups (ten or more members) to have two directors.

4. **Finish the video production proposal, script, and storyboard.** If a group has not done so, it should now be working together under its producer and director to complete the Video Production Proposal, write a script, and create a storyboard. Lots of work here! Make sure producers keep every member of their team busy.

5. **Assign the rest of the video crew.** Once you have accepted and approved a group's Video Production Proposal, the director can begin to assign crew duties. A group may want to hold auditions. (The director decides! The producer can override the director, but discourage this.) In the next lesson, groups will choose lighting, sound, and graphics for their videos. The video is becoming a reality!

LESSON 6
ORGANIZING FOR VIDEO PRODUCTION

TEACHER'S OBJECTIVES

- to assist students in the final preparations for their video productions
- to outline procedures and techniques in creating graphics
- to demonstrate correct and effective techniques for lighting and sound
- to assist in final rehearsals and run-throughs

STUDENTS' OBJECTIVES

- to complete the initial planning and revise the Video Production Proposal
- to create effective graphics for the production
- to use sound and lighting correctly
- to participate effectively in the group's production

FUNDAMENTALS

Students are now working enthusiastically on their productions. Your role is to direct traffic. Encourage producers and directors to be responsible for involving each member of their crew. You will be meeting with lighting and sound technicians to show them basic techniques.

THE TEACHER WILL NEED TO KNOW

Creating graphics for a video production can be quite simple. The important thing to remember is to leave plenty of space around the edges of the paper or other material so the camera does not record anything beyond the edges. When my students use poster board or butcher paper, I ask them to leave at least three inches around the edges, and often that is not enough. Investigate various options for introducing graphics in a video: use magnetic letters on a board, use a felt board, tape letters to a wall (brick is a neat texture), or use cutout letters lit from behind (see "Graphics," page 27). Have fun with it!

Sound and lighting also need not be overwhelming, particularly if the production is simple. I have always found at least one student who preferred to do lights or sound over anything else. Often this student could handle lights and sound for every video production with a few willing assistants. (Don't be surprised if this person is a girl!)

For simple lighting, you can buy inexpensive "scoop" lights, a metal cone, and a clip. These cast a harsh glare, but they are fine for beginning video productions. Be sure to use heavy-duty extension cords! (See "Lighting," page 26, and "Sound," page 26, for more information.)

Remind students to *always point the camera away from the sun or lights! Direct light will damage the lens.*

STUDENTS WILL NEED TO KNOW

By now students should have completed their scripts and storyboards, and should understand basic camera terminology. They should understand how to use paints, paper, glue, or whatever else they will use for their graphics.

The sound and light people should have a basic understanding of electricity, the use of wires, connections, recordings, and so forth. Remember, you do not need experts yet. This is a learning experience!

MATERIALS

- lights (at least two scoop lights)
- white poster board for "bouncing" light on the set
- necessary sound equipment (microphones, appropriate jacks, cord)
- materials for graphics
- optional: transparencies of lettering styles

VOCABULARY

Back light
Bouncing light
Graphics
Fill light
Key light

PROCEDURES

Preparation: Students will require little preparation now. Most of them will be so excited you will need to hold them back to ensure a better production. Keep their attention on details and insist that no job be rushed. Circulate among the groups and make sure everyone has something to do.

1. **Revise and update the Video Production Proposal.** The main purpose of this lesson is for groups to make sure their Video Production Proposals reflect what they want their tape to be. Make sure at least part of each group is at work keeping its proposal current.

2. **Define the masking area for graphics.** Help students begin their graphics. If possible, use the camera to show that the image area on the screen is not square. Standard monitors are four units across and three units down. Point out that if students extend their writing or drawing to the edges of the background, the edges of the background and beyond will show on the screen. To guard against this, they should "mask" an area at least three inches wide all the way around the background. The more centered the graphic, the better.

3. **Recognize contrast problems.** Inform students that too much contrast in their graphics can actually damage the camera. Avoid using black with white, for example, or any other strongly contrasting colors.

4. **Identify graphics options.** Discuss with students the variety of options available for graphics. They can use a variety of letters, background materials, or lighting. Aluminum foil can make an interesting graphic (watch lighting, though), as well as burlap or backlit lettering. Try cutting graphics out of posterboard and using fishline to "fly" them in front of the camera or use press-type, computer-generated graphics, or other commercially available lettering. Pan across the graphic or tilt the poster up or down. Be creative!

Remind the groups to anticipate and list every graphic, including ones such as "The next day . . . " or "Meanwhile . . . "

I use a book of lettering styles to create transparencies of various lettering types. Students can trace the style they choose onto paper, cardboard, or the chalkboard. They can vary sizes and styles easily. Try it!

5. **Anticipate sound and lighting needs.** At this time you should have all groups of students working happily on some aspect of a video production (costumes, makeup, graphics, scripts, props, rehearsals). You will need to meet with the lighting people to explain the rudiments of lighting. You may also need to meet with the sound people if you have special audio needs in a particular video.

Ask the lighting and sound people to set up a few test situations and tape them, then let the technicians evaluate their tape with the director or producer. Which is most effective? Ask the lighting and sound people to go on location and look for potential problems. The big courtroom scene of one of my classes was almost wrecked because the church we were using took down the drapes to clean on the day we came to tape, and huge beams of sunlight wreaked havoc with our camera. What will the natural lighting and sound be like on the day and at the time you plan to tape? Will the school bus pull up during the exciting conclusion? Will the lunch bell ring just as the interview begins? Will the audience see the cameraperson's shadow? You cannot overplan! But remember that the video process itself often suggests solutions—it is wonderfully adaptable!

This lesson is the heart of the production. Keep everyone involved and you will find this and the next lesson the most rewarding sessions.

LESSON 7
THE PRODUCTION!

TEACHER'S OBJECTIVES

- to help groups tape a video production
- to provide feedback as requested or necessary to maintain or improve the quality of students' productions
- to continue to guide groups toward the completion of their productions

STUDENTS' OBJECTIVES

- to participate constructively in the taping of a video production

FUNDAMENTALS

Most students feel that this session is the climax of everything that has gone before. Help them keep their perspective by reminding them that this lesson is only part of the iceberg—a small part of a much larger whole. If their planning has been productive, then this session will be productive.

You may find you feel left out of this session. If your class is really hard at work and working well together, congratulations! They have been taught very well. But not every class has the maturity to work well together, or the ambience to encourage it, so you can still play a positive role by continuing to guide the groups in their work.

Continue to keep your objectivity in case students lose theirs.

Remember, scenes may need to be shot out of sequence to use your facilities and equipment most effectively. In addition, different groups may need to share equipment and locations. Ask directors and crews to work to achieve the most effective use of the equipment in the time you have.

At this point, it is helpful to enlist the aid of another teacher or parent to keep an eye on students not directly involved. Plan to have some activities ready or ask students to bring materials to keep themselves occupied. A lot of time in production is spent simply waiting. Be prepared.

THE TEACHER WILL NEED TO KNOW

It always takes longer than you think! One group of students estimated that it took them seven hours of recording to get seven minutes of final tape. You will always want more time! Plan for this! My students have never finished within their schedule. We always wanted to do more or do over what we had already done.

Know when to stop. You must stop sometime. Plan on it. And let the students know that stopping date.

STUDENTS WILL NEED TO KNOW

Students should be ready for just about anything. You've done a fine job! Some groups may have special needs, however. Work with them to find solutions to their problems. Although this is not network television, challenge students to find creative ways to get the effects they want!

MATERIALS

Each group should have a blank videotape for recording their production. Students will also need whatever props, materials, costumes, and so forth they listed in their Video Production Proposals. Expect that someone will forget something. It happens. Become a creative problem solver. If you can borrow equipment *compatible with yours,* do it! Have more than one camera at a time!

PROCEDURES

Preparation: Make sure all equipment is collected and ready and have all materials on location. Bring extra extension cords and light bulbs!

If students are planning to edit, be sure they break down the scenes and arrange them so that all scenes at one location are shot at the same time. If they are taping the video in sequence, of course they cannot break down the scenes. If more than one group plan to use the same location, ask them to be ready so they can begin to tape at that location as soon as the first group is done.

Make sure your video recorder is recording at the fastest speed! High-quality editing equipment can edit only material recorded at the fastest speed. Besides, the fastest speed records the highest quality video and audio.

Do not allow groups to view what they have taped at this point unless another group is using the recording equipment.

1. **Roll the tape!** Make sure everyone is involved as much as possible. Here is where producers and directors can shine. Support them in their endeavors. Be sure students are following the correct procedures, especially the countdown discussed in lesson 3. Let each tape run for one minute before you start recording. At the beginning of each take, the sound person or the director says, "Scene X, take X," just after the countdown and just before the action begins. These statements helps enor-mously later on. Be sure the person is close enough to the microphone to be heard.

   Remember to tape your graphics! Try taping them all at the beginning, unless you are taping in sequence.

2. **Evaluate the productions.** Allow time at the end of the session to view what was recorded. Run each tape through completely with pauses, countdowns, mistakes, retakes, and so forth. This process is always fun and illuminating.

   You may not need to schedule another taping session!

   Ask students to critique the tapes informally. Remind them to keep comments constructive!

PRODUCTION NOTES

LESSON 8
LOGGING AND EDITING ROUGH FOOTAGE

TEACHER'S OBJECTIVES

- to help students log their taped scenes
- to assist students in the effective selection and sequencing of desired scenes
- to demonstrate effective editing techniques

STUDENTS' OBJECTIVES

- to correctly log each scene in a videotape
- to order each scene in the correct sequence to complete a video

FUNDAMENTALS

Students should have completed their taping. In this session, they will log the takes of each scene—watch the tape and time the scene or record counter numbers—and select which scenes to put together into a finished video. You should show all students how to log. After you have taught them, any student can log the actual videotape, but you will find it more efficient to ask the producer, director, and/or cameraperson to log.

You should also show all students how to edit, if possible. Editing can be tricky. If you know someone in the video field, this may be the time to enlist his or her help. When you help students actually edit their videotapes, however, do so with only the producer, director, and possibly the cameraperson of each video. When decisions have to be made (for example, cutting an entire scene because it is too long or too poorly done), you will want to avoid any personality conflicts or claims of favoritism. Once again, decisions made by the people present at the editing session should be considered final.

Of course, if you want to create the job of editor, now is the chance! Remember to name the editor in the credits.

If a group taped everything in order, they don't have to edit and can go right on to the next lesson.

THE TEACHER WILL NEED TO KNOW

Logging a videotape can be simple. Use the Edit Log form in the appendix (page 86) to note the counter numbers at the beginning and end of each scene. Have students note comments about each scene as they watch, for example, "too loud," "poor lighting," "best shot." Pause after each scene to allow them time to record this information.

Each video recorder counter works differently, so try to use the same VCR for all the logging. To begin logging, rewind the tape and set the counter at zero. If you rewind a tape you have started to log or stop and try to start over again, your counter numbers may be slightly off. This is normal.

See "Editing," page 29, for editing procedures.

STUDENTS WILL NEED TO KNOW

- how to use a VCR to view a tape
- how to set the counter on the VCR to zero

MATERIALS

- a VCR for viewing and logging tapes
- copies of the Edit Log form
- editing equipment, access to editing equipment, or two VCRs
- blank videotapes to edit onto

VOCABULARY

Edit
Log

PROCEDURES

Preparation: Inform students that this step produces the finished product. This is where all the hard work pays off. Editing takes time, so plan for it.

1. **Correctly log each take of each scene.** Since each student should learn how to log, take a few minutes to teach the process. Insert the videotape into the VCR and make sure the VCR counters are at 0000. Give each student an Edit Log form.

Explain to students that they should record the "in" counter number, the one that the scene begins with, in the first column. They should record the "out" counter number, the one that the scene ends with, in the second column. In the large third column, students should note an identifying feature such as scene and take number, or an opening line or action that takes place in the scene. Also, ask students to note information about the quality of the scene such as "excellent effect," "poor lighting here," or "car noise too loud." They should star the best take of each scene. (You can now see the value of the countdown before each scene, as well as the "scene 5, take 2" information recorded at the beginning of each take.)

Begin playing the tape and ask students to log each take of each scene. Stop the tape at intervals and ask students to evaluate what they have logged. Which was the best take? Why? Point out subtle differences between takes or problems or even advantages of one over the other. Praise effective takes. Be sure to analyze them for their effectiveness.

After a while you will stop logging and leave the rest for your producer/director team. Remind them to rewind the tape and set the counters at 0000 if they start from the beginning (which they must do if the VCR is used by another group and the counter numbers are changed).

2. **Order the best choice of each scene in the correct sequence.** Students can manipulate their logging information in several ways to put it in a workable order for editing:

- They can write each logged scene on a slip of paper or index card, complete with all pertinent information such as counter numbers and notes to the editing group ("cut scene after Damien falls" or "need music here"). Cards are particularly helpful because they can be ordered and reordered. They can also be helpful if you are using some takes in another production—you get double duty for them. They can be awkward and easily dropped, however, so be careful if you use this method.

- Students may prefer to jot their order of preference on another sheet. Although much easier to use initially, this can lead to problems later if the sequence must be changed, notes added, and so forth.

Using an appropriate method, students should select the best take of each scene and note these takes in the order they want for the final production. Students should begin to get some idea of the flow of the final tape. Now is also a good time to discuss any problems with the final production they can foresee. It is common for students to feel they must retape some scenes or add others. If possible, allow them this luxury. Perhaps you can add extra time to the schedule.

3. **Use effective video editing techniques.** You will probably have to use two VCRs to produce a passable edit; this option may be sufficient for your needs at this time.

If you have access to editing equipment, so much the better, although this equipment is usually expensive, and students may need to direct a technician instead of working with the equipment themselves.

In many large cities, video production labs will rent their video editing equipment, but you must use it in their facility. If travel is no problem, you may want to look into this option. Remember your local university or college. The department of teleproduction or media may be willing to let you use their equipment.

Also inquire if a community cable corporation has been established to facilitate citizens' involvement in producing video material for public access channels. In many larger cities, such organizations provide equipment free of charge to interested individuals. Investigate your options!

When you are finished editing, one important step remains: evaluation.

OPTIONAL ASSIGNMENT

An excellent activity to do before students begin editing their own tapes is for you to have a prepared tape of rough footage and ask each student to assemble it into a finished production. Each student will need access to editing equipment. It is time consuming, so it is best done as homework or as an outside assignment if possible.

LESSON 9
EVALUATION, STUDENT-STYLE

TEACHER'S OBJECTIVES
- to direct students in the evaluation of their video production
- to evaluate students' productions, performance, and participation
- to provide feedback to students about their productions, performance, and participation

STUDENTS' OBJECTIVES
- to recall the Criteria for Evaluation chart from lesson 1
- to recall the elements of a video production: theme, setting, plot, mood, characterization, layering
- to evaluate the completed video productions according to the Criteria for Evaluation chart

FUNDAMENTALS
After everyone has watched the videos at least three times, there is one important step that students must complete. For maximum growth and learning from this experience, students must evaluate their work. Evaluation forces them to see where they were and what they have done to get where they are now. You will find that some students have already analyzed the productions and have made some rudimentary observations. You need to formalize these comments through class discussion.

Remember lesson 1? If you wondered why students needed to construct a Criteria for Evaluation chart, now you know. They can finally use their own criteria on themselves. They can become their own critics.

STUDENTS WILL NEED TO
- have finished their editing

MATERIALS
- the Criteria for Evaluation chart created in lesson 1
- a chalkboard and chalk
- a VCR and students' completed tapes

VOCABULARY

From Lesson 1, review

Characterization

Layering

Mood

Plot

Setting

Theme

PROCEDURES

Preparation: Tell students that they will begin to see and understand their video productions in new ways after today's lesson.

1. **Ask students to recall the elements of a dramatic work.** Write the elements on the chalkboard as the students name them: theme, setting, plot, mood, characterization, layering. Summarize each element quickly.

2. **Identify the elements of each video production.** Construct a chart on the chalkboard and ask students to identify each element in each video. Write each element as it is identified. If students worked in groups, you might want each group to meet and work through these steps.

3. **Point out the posted Criteria for Evaluation chart students constructed in lesson 1.** Remind students how they applied these criteria to evaluate their favorite television shows.

4. **Evaluate the video productions using the Criteria for Evaluation.** Ask students to evaluate each video production using their Criteria for Evaluation. They may discover that they need to update their criteria in light of their experience. Hooray! You might want students to compose a written review of each production according to the Criteria for Evaluation. Make sure each student understands the strengths and weaknesses of each production.

If you find you have a production that is notoriously weak, have that production group analyze their work aloud for the class. Ask them to concentrate on what was effective and what was ineffective. (Questions you might ask: What was the weakest spot in the production? What would have improved the production? What would you keep in the production? Analyze the production in terms of its elements. What have you learned that you can use more effectively in your next production?) This technique is also valuable with a production group whose video was very effective. You might want to videotape the analysis of the highly successful group to show in successive years.

Briefly discuss the use of layering in the video productions. Again, stress the point that successful video productions depend on careful thought, preparation, and creativity to structure their effects to the best end. No successful production simply happens. It is planned.

You may want to look at other videos, even the ones you looked at in lesson 1, to see how student reviews have changed.

APPENDIXES

Appendix A
WAYS TO USE
VIDEO IN SCHOOLS
Administration

- prepare orientation tapes
- tape student council meetings
- tape sample parent-teacher interviews
- document each year with a video yearbook
- use clips from classroom activities at Open House
- share examples of teaching techniques

Art

- demonstrate techniques (close-ups especially valuable)
- tape exhibits to share with other schools or grades
- tape museum tours to share with others
- introduce new art media
- bring local architecture into classroom
- illustrate perspective, contrast, shadow, and other details

FIG.1   FIG.2   FIG.3

Business

- tape an actual job interview
- demonstrate special techniques (typing, for example)
- demonstrate repair techniques
- interview business people
- tape "on-the-job" documentaries

Driver Training

- demonstrate correct driving techniques
- demonstrate parking, changing a tire, and other activities
- illustrate traffic hazards
- conduct interviews with law personnel, accident victims, and so forth

English

- dramatize stories, myths, plays, poetry
- stage interviews with legendary people
- introduce and demonstrate library techniques
- tape oral readings and presentations for evaluation
- tape students reading books for younger students
- tape students recommending books to younger students

Foreign Language

- tape correct pronunciations and expressions
- tape field trips to plays, countries, cultural events
- tape interviews with people speaking foreign languages
- use animation to demonstrate sounds

General Classroom Teaching

- tape classroom activities for Open House or PTA meetings
- tape special programs to share with class
- document a year's activities for orientation next year
- tape lessons for absent students
- tape introductory lessons to avoid repetition
- tape close-up demonstrations of great detail for general class viewing
- create commercials for some aspect of school

Health

- demonstrate first aid
- analyze proper health techniques: posture, nutrition, movement, and so forth
- document incidents of drug or alcohol abuse
- illustrate recognition, prevention, and treatment of disease

Science

- demonstrate scientific method
- detail experiments, pause to hypothesize results
- document results of experiments
- share science activities with other classes
- document results for science fairs
- share special programs
- illustrate complex, unsafe, or costly experiments

Social Studies

- document field trips
- focus on maps, graphs, diagrams, charts
- dramatize historical events
- record interviews with local resource people
- create "news" programs
- stage interviews

Speech and Theater

- tape student rehearsals
- replay taped performances for evaluation
- document performances
- tape debate techniques
- tape dress rehearsals
- demonstrate physical and audio formation of sounds

Sports

- tape practices for instruction
- tape games or events

Appendix B
MATERIALS FOR THE CLASSROOM
Graphics

The art resource teacher in your school can be a wonderful source of information for ways and means of producing graphics for your video production. Consult him or her with technical questions about materials and media, how to use various adhesives, and how to choose color for maximum impact. If your school has an art room, perhaps you could make arrangement to use it as working space for creating graphics. If some of your students are artistically inclined, perhaps they could work with the art teacher. Be sure to arrange for using the space and get permission to use tools and materials!

A visit to your local art or office supply store will give you a wide choice of materials and methods for producing type. Commercially produced press-on and pressure-sensitive letters are available in may typestyles, sizes, colors, and materials. Some are removable and some are permanent. Many art suppliers offer a catalog of available typestyles that makes a good reference for your classroom. You can also make enlarged photocopies of pages from these catalogs and cut and paste the letters on white paper.

If you have access to a computer either in your home or at school, consider using computer-generated graphics. Many programs are available that allow you to set up an entire page with the letters exactly where you want them in the frame (centered or lines up on the left with plenty of white space around the edges). Some computers allow a wide choice of fonts and sizes, with many options for layout and even graphics (such as the one that produced this book!). Photocopy outlets offer self-serve computer time, with high-quality laser output, at a reasonable cost. Explore all your options. Consult the resource people at your school, and don't forget the parents!

Appendix C
DIRECTING NONPROFESSIONAL TALENT

As a teacher, you will be working with nonprofessional talent almost exclusively. Therefore, you have to prepare more and spend a bit more time and effort on "maintenance" (that is, crowd control) than professionals do.

You have decisions to make. Do you want this to be a learning experience or do you want your video to be the best possible? If it's a learning experience, let your student producer and director(s) handle the talent and the situations; you just shepherd the fringes. If you want the best, then you'll need to be more involved. No matter which direction you take, you'll have to be sure you and your students do the following:

First, prepare!! Nothing will compensate for inadequate preparation. Set up before the talent arrives. Make sure you have extra copies of scripts, tapes, essential props. Of course, you can delegate this job to your producers and directors. Plan a schedule so everyone is occupied a majority of the time. Idle hands . . . you know!

Help the talent prepare. Give them scripts ahead of time. Be clear about who's doing what job: costumes, props, makeup, effects. You will spend a lot of time in preproduction, and you should.

Relax the talent. They will be nervous. Remind them that you will be editing material to make them look good. Go over again what you want them to do, and then *rehearse!* Ask the director and producer to run a rehearsal as if it were the real thing. Don't allow talking, moving, and so on offstage while students are rehearsing. In fact, you might want to tape the rehearsal, and then watch it. Coach the talent if necessary. Make sure they understand the purpose of lighting, sound equipment, angles, and so on. Tell them clearly if you want them to look into the camera or not, and when.

A common problem is talent's apparent lack of energy in the final product. Encourage them to "be bigger" in their actions and even to "show too much energy" or "come on too strong." These directions may produce the balanced energy that you need.

Allow no prima donnas! The talent is simply hired help. They do not run the production or make any decisions other than personal interpretation, and possibly not even that! Listen to their ideas about interpretation, but make your own decisions. Expect them to know their lines, their time schedules, and the blocking (even though they won't!)

Ultimately, the responsibility is yours for the quality of the final product, and the talent does not have your perspective. As talent, they are subordinate to you in decision making, and must abide by your decisions. Producer and director run the show!! (As the teacher and "executive producer" be sure to support this hierarchy to avoid anarchy.)

The decision to replace talent is yours, the director's, and producer's. Handle any personnel decisions fairly and professionally. Remind

your producer and director that removing talent or anyone on staff is also a political move and may have repercussions, affecting the production. Weigh all decisions carefully.

Finally, don't allow the talent to watch the tape until after editing. If they are nervous, watching themselves only increases their self-awareness. Allow only the producer and director viewing privileges during taping to make any decisions that need to be made.

Nonprofessional talent is often refreshing. Enjoy them!

Appendix D
STUDENT SKILL CHART
Students should acquire the following skills at each stage of video production:

Preproduction
- Identify theme, plot, setting, characterization, mood.
- Analyze these elements for relationships.
- Construct character analyses.

Production
- Operate camera: turn on/off, record/pause, zoom in/out, pan, tilt, dolly, truck.
- Execute camera shots: ECU, CU, MS, LS.
- Frame shots: use rule of thirds, place subject's eyes two-thirds of the way up screen, allow for head room and talking space.
- Directing cues and gestures: *stand by; roll tape;* counting *"5, 4, 3, 2, 1"; action;* countdown at end of scene *"5, 4, 3, 2, 1—Cut!"*
- Use constructive feedback to guide talent and crew during scenes.

Postproduction

- Log tapes
- Structure scenes into appropriate sequence for finished video.
- Edit scenes into appropriate sequence.
- Evaluate finished video.

Peripherals

Graphics

- Plan and construct simple graphics.
- Use prepared graphics.
- Construct simple graphics according to plans.
- Plan and construct special effects graphics.

Lights

- Create and use simple lighting plans.
- Create and use special effects lighting.

Sound

- Use given sound equipment.
- Create and use simple audio plans.
- Create and use special audio effects.

Costumes/Set

- Create and use simple costumes and set designs.
- Create and use special effects in costumes and set designs.

Appendix E
SUGGESTIONS FOR POSITIVE FEEDBACK

page 21

A sample statement of praise. "Look how Diane really had a sense for color in this shot—the way the straw flowers and the child's hair look together."

page 49

"It was teamwork that paid off here—your director, Marcia, cued Rob the cameraperson to go to the medium shot and give Barbara the guest more looking room—see how the shot is balanced now?"

page 51

"Let's look for the spot where Steve changes the frame—notice any difference? Does this work better?"

page 54

Regarding brainstorming, encourage participation. Help the group avoid judgment and avoid discussion of brainstormed ideas for the moment. "It looks like Mark wants to say something. What's your idea?"

page 55

Be firm about more thought in simplistic videos. "Yes, we see violence on TV a lot. What we're after here are your ideas about what stories you want to tell with video. What do you like doing yourself? Our video project is for your new ideas. Try to do something we haven't seen done before. What stories in real life have meant the most to you?"

page 73

"Let's find out more about the planning that went into this effective piece. George's team revised their production plan several times before they were satisfied with it.

Remember their great scene under the bleachers? That was an idea that came up only after they taped how they originally planned it. This group was not afraid to make changes to make their piece better. Also, it was Sarah the cameraperson's idea for the bleacher shot and her director, Melissa, was receptive to it.

Appendix F
SAMPLE SCRIPT AND STORYBOARD SHEETS
Video Column Suggestions

- Place camera directions in the video column, spaced alongside the corresponding audio directions.
- Use ALL CAPITAL LETTERS and single spacing in camera directions.
- Use quotation marks and upper- and lowercase letters for titles and graphics.
- Leave several lines of space between video descriptions.

Audio Column Suggestions

- Identify the speaker for all spoken lines when beginning each speech and after each interruption.
- Use underlined capital letters for the speaker's name. Put the name on a line by itself with a colon.
- Use upper- and lower-case letters for words to be spoken.
- Indicate voiceovers or narration with parentheses.
- Directions to talent—on or off camera—appear in the audio column.
- Sound cues are separate from speech.

SCRIPT SHEET

Program _____

Producer/Director _____

VIDEO	AUDIO
FADE IN	**HOST:**
	Welcome to A.M. People. I'm Linda Hostess and with me today is Samson Smith, a new student in our class.
ZOOM OUT TO 2 SHOT OF HOST AND GUEST	TELL me, Samson, what do you like most about our class, what do you do in our class, and what encouraged you to say "yes" to being in video production?
CU OF GUEST	**GUEST:**
	In video production we do interesting things. We work with cameras and equipment. We learn to do video in an exciting way. We do it ourselves! I like that!
2 SHOT OF HOST AND GUEST	**HOST:**
	Okay, I think you've answered most of my questions. Audience, if you have any questions, please call 1-800-V-I-D-E-O. Thank you for coming, Samson.
ZOOM IN TO CU OF HOST	And Thank you for watching. Stay with us, because after this commercial we'll interview Wally the Gorilla.
FADE TO BLACK	

STORYBOARD SHEET

Copies can be made of the original

Program _____

Producer/Director _____

FADE IN / ZOOM OUT TO 2 SHOT OF (H)+(G)

AUDIO

HOST: Welcome to A.M. People. I'm Linda Hostess and with me today is Samson Smith, a new student in our class.

CU of GUEST

AUDIO H: tell me, Samson, what do you like about our class, what do you do in our class and what encouraged you to say "yes" to being in video production?

AUDIO GUEST: IN video production we do interesting Things. We work with cameras and equipment. We learn to do video in an exciting way: We do it ourselves! I like that.

2 SHOT OF (H)+(G) / ZOOM IN TO CU OF (H)

AUDIO H: Okay, I think you've answered most of my questions. Audience, if you have any questions, Please call 1-800-V-I-D-E-O. Thank you for coming, Samson.

FADE TO BLACK

AUDIO H: AND THANK you for watching. Stay with us, because after this commercial we'll interview Wally the Gorilla

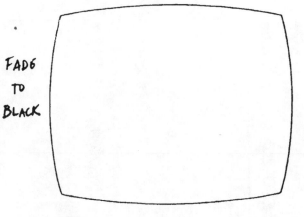

AUDIO

82

Appendix G

BLANK FORMS

SCRIPT SHEET

Program

Producer/Director

Video	Audio

Producer/Director

Audio

Audio

Audio

Audio

Audio

Audio

KidVid, © 2000 Zephyr Press, Tucson, Arizona.

EDIT LOG

Counter Number	Audio/Video Cue		
	In		Out

Appendix H
OPTIONAL ACTIVITIES: ENHANCING VIDEO SKILLS

You can use these exercises to evaluate students' skills or to help them improve their skills. You can also use the exercises as models to create your own. They will also help your students gain experience and confidence with the equipment.

Microphone Round Robin

This activity is intended to increase your students' familiarity with a variety of audio recording devices. Remember, even microphones within a category—shotgun mikes, for example—will vary in quality. Thus, this exercise will not necessarily evaluate which type of mike is better, but which individual mike works best in a given situation.

Collect a variety of microphones: lavaliere mike (small clip-on like the one newscasters use), desktop mike (on a stand a la *The Tonight Show* or flat), shotgun mike (long thin mike used to aim at a more distant sound source), inexpensive mike (the kind you get with a cheap tape recorder), remote mike (does not connect to the camera, but to a radio transmitter; you plug a receiver into the camcorder).

Choose one microphone you have collected; write the brand name and the type on a sheet of paper (for example, Sony mike that came with camcorder). Under that, list the following items, leaving a space for response after each:

Fidelity
How realistic is the sound?

Is the voice deep or flat?

Can you hear breathing?

Does it distort any letters (p and b are common distortions)?

Frequency Response
Does it pick up highs and lows equally well?

If not, which does it pick up better?

Pickup Pattern
Does it pick up only in front?

Only on the sides?

All around?

Handling Characteristics
Is it lightweight?

Small?

Sensitive?

Does it pick up its own noise when you move it?

Best Use
In what recording situations would this mike be most effective?

Outdoors?

Indoors?

Up close?

Far away?

To record music?

Speaking voices only?

Next, use that mike to record a group member's voice on your videotape. The person speaking should state what kind of mike you are using for the test, then move around to test the pickup pattern (see chart). The person holding the mike should shake it gently occasionally to determine its handling characteristics (see chart). Repeat the test with several other mikes.

When the test is done, play back the tape and listen carefully for subtle differences between the mikes. Fill in the answers to the questions on your chart.

Video Skills Exercise

Provide students with three items, one a chair or box, and the other two toys or some unique objects. Students complete the shots in the following order:

1. Write your name on a piece of paper or card; videotape the card so your name is clearly seen. Hold the shot for 5 to 10 seconds.
2. Compose a shot using one of the two items on the chair or box. Place the other item off to the side on the same level as the first. Tape the chair shot for 5 to 10 seconds.
3. Pan carefully to the other item placed off to the side. Tape that shot for 5 to 10 seconds.
4. Pan back to the original item. Tape for 3 to 4 seconds. Stop taping. Move the second item to the floor beneath the first item.
5. Begin taping again. Tape the chair shot for 5 to 10 seconds. Tilt the camera down from the top item to the bottom item. Tape for 5 to 10 seconds.
6. Zoom in, then out on the item. Stop taping and move the top item over to the side.
7. Begin taping again and simultaneously tilt and pan to the top object. Tape the top object for 5 to 10 seconds. Stop taping.

VIDEO SKILLS EVALUATION FORM

1. The items were arranged in an interesting fashion.

   1 2 3 4 5

2. The opening shot is clear, in focus, and steady.

   1 2 3 4 5

3. The camera pans are steady and smooth.

   1 2 3 4 5

4. The camera tilts are steady and smooth.

   1 2 3 4 5

5. The camera zooms are steady and smooth.

   1 2 3 4 5

6. The simultaneous tilt and pan are steady and smooth.

   1 2 3 4 5

7. The final shot is clear, in focus, and steady.

   1 2 3 4 5

KidVid, © 2000 Zephyr Press, Tucson, Arizona.

Scavenger Hunt

A video scavenger hunt can be a fun, exciting way for students to practice video skills. Teams of students videotape items from a list during a specific time period and with specific limitations.

You may not have enough equipment for the teams to share. In that case, ask students to bring in camcorders from home. Check with your administrators to determine your district's policy on using borrowed equipment. Be sure to obtain parental permission, of course. And to eliminate possible difficulties, establish a policy that those students who bring in camcorders are the *only* students allowed to operate them.

If you are doing the hunt at school, be sure to inform others in your school about your project so they will be expecting some interruptions. If some teachers do not want to participate, then make sure your students know not to try to get anything from those classrooms. In addition, to make sure the students keep disruptions to a minimum, tell participating teachers that they have the privilege to request a card from any team who disturbs them unnecessarily or to a great degree. They get to be the judge of what is disruptive. The offending students will give them an index card with their team name on it, and you will have a box to collect the cards in your classroom. The teacher sends someone to deliver the card to the box, and at the end of the project, you will deduct points for each card from that team's total score.

I have included sample scavenger lists from a variety of situations. Adapt them to your own situation and time frame. You can use this exercise outdoors, in a downtown public arena—wherever your imagination and safety leads you. I've done it all over a university, in a small town's shopping area, a mall. Be sure to check out the place first to establish physical limitations ("you may not go beyond the automotive store"), to help you personalize the list to the site, and to make sure the authorities know of this activity and don't disapprove.

To prepare, make sure your students can operate the camcorder, even if their skills are basic. If you have tapes of scavenger hunts from preceding classes, show them and critique them: "See how they forgot to check if the camcorder had stopped recording? Now we have 20 minutes of a hanging video camera as they walk!" "Look at the angle they used there!"

Divide the class into three- to four-person teams. Give each team one videotape. Distribute the scavenger lists. Give each team a certain number of index cards—say, four—with their names or a team name listed on them. Tell them that, if they disturb a class, the teacher can ask for a card and send someone to place the card in the box in your room. You will deduct points from the team's total for each card. If students run out of cards (disturb more than four teachers, say), then they are disqualified.

Students will have to make some decisions about taking risks and accept blame or credit graciously. For example, if they ask a teacher who is alone in his room to whistle "Dixie" for them, it is less likely he will think it is a disturbance than a teacher who is in the middle of explaining the periodic chart. However, remind them that the teacher gets to decide if something is a disturbance. During the taping, wander the assigned site to make sure students are adhering to the rules.

If possible, arrange to have at least 2 monitors and VCRs and some fun music to accompany the playback. Play more than one tape at the same time. The students enjoy the "slide show video" images playing on side-by-side monitors at the same time. Critique each team orally during the viewing and afterward on paper. Keep feedback constructive and positive; praise creative and responsible work lavishly.

Basic Scavenger Hunt

A total of 450 points is possible. Points will be deducted for unsportsmanlike conduct (–200 points per instance); misuse of equipment, property, or student (–200 points per instance); any other infraction of the rules as judged by the instructors (–25 points per instance); any index cards returned from other teachers (–25 points per card); and going outside the building (–50 points per instance).

Keep each shot as tight as possible!!

Don't forget your 5-second count before and after you tape!

Look to be sure you've stopped taping!

Points

75 points for taping the starting countdown and clap

25 points for introducing each member of your team (or self)

10 points for each of the following in any order, taped separately—no combinations!

- something moving you follow for 5 seconds
- a bird
- a ball bouncing
- someone over age 50
- a phone ringing
- the colors red, yellow, and blue together

- someone clapping hands and whistling "Dixie"
- a picture postcard
- running water
- something that sparkles
- an *Exit* sign
- someone telling a joke
- someone brushing another person's hair
- something light and dark at the same time
- an ant's eye view of something
- the front page of today's newspaper
- someone saying "May I help you?"
- someone in uniform
- bare feet
- a reflection
- someone on a bike or motorbike
- a flag
- someone playing a game
- a smile with braces
- a floral display

25 points for taping the 3-minute warning signal

75 points for taping final countdown and clap.

Advanced Video Scavenger Hunt

A total of 400 points is possible. Points will be deducted for unsportsmanlike conduct (–200 points per instance); misuse of equipment or property (–200 points per instance); going outside the building (–50 points per instance); any other infraction of the rules as judged by the instructors (–25 points per instance); any index cards returned from other teachers (–25 points per card).

Combinations of shots are allowed.

Points

25 points for taping teacher's countdown and bell to start

10 points for each of the following in any order

- water running
- bell ringing
- reflection shot
- "color bars," something with red, blue, and yellow
- student working in hall (5 points if student sees you)
- CU of working clock
- CU of someone snapping fingers
- door closing
- other video crew videotaping
- car going by school outside

- school bus
- empty classroom
- bench
- plant
- name of school
- key swinging
- trophy (5 points extra if a name is clearly seen)
- wooden sign
- light that isn't working
- the words *Getting Started*
- *reserved* sign
- someone singing
- *All visitors report to Main Office* sign
- introducing each member of the team
- empty hallway
- girl smiling
- person gargling water at fountain
- someone going up stairs
- *No smoking* sign
- *Caution Asbestos Hazard* sign

25 points for taping the warning bell

50 points for taping the ending bell

Creative Connection Scavenger Hunt

A total of 500 points is possible. Points will be deducted for unsportsmanlike conduct (–200 points per instance); misuse of equipment or property (–200 points per instance); going outside the building (–50 points per instance); any other infraction of the rules as judged by the instructors (–25 points per instance); any index cards returned from other teachers (–25 points per card).

KidVid, © 2000 Zephyr Press, Tucson, Arizona

Points

75 points for taping the starting whistle

25 points for introducing each member of the team

10 points for each of the following, taped separately—no combinations!

- old person
- phone ringing
- colors red, blue, and yellow together
- student clapping hands and whistling "Dixie"
- price of fries
- revolving door
- school postcard
- running water
- something that sparkles
- *Exit* sign
- school bus pulling away
- spiral staircase from an unusual angle
- person sleeping
- someone telling a joke

- an animal
- something light and dark at the same time
- ant's eye view of something
- today's date
- polka dots
- someone saying "May I help you?"
- school bag in motion
- a beautiful person from the back
- flag
- someone in uniform
- something flying, folding, or falling
- bare feet
- ball bouncing
- a smile with braces
- someone playing a game
- someone brushing another person's hair

25 points for taping 5-minute warning whistle

75 points for taping final countdown and whistle

Additional Challenges

You can create an evaluation format similar to the one on page 90 for these exercises.

1. Students can create two separate videos for playing on two monitors placed side by side. They might show, for example, a ball that rolls across and off one screen, then appears a second later to roll across the other screen. The effect is that the ball seems to roll across the empty space between the monitors. This technique involves an awareness of time and space that can really be fun for students who would enjoy the challenge.

2. Students can practice their editing skills by taping video over a prerecorded audio track. They can use a popular song, script a story based on their interpretation of the song, and videotape the story, taping the audio onto the track as well.

Appendix I
VIDEO PRODUCTION PROPOSAL

Complete each section thoroughly and get your teacher's approval for your proposal before you begin production. Use another sheet of paper if necessary.

I. Analysis of Intended Audience

Describe a single member of your audience as thoroughly as possible. Think about age, sex, educational level, socioeconomic status, and so forth. This section will help you with step II and will provide a solid basis for developing the remaining steps.

II. Statement of Purpose of the Production.

What is the purpose of this video? What is it you want the viewer to have after seeing your video that he or she didn't have before? What will be your point of view?

III. Summary of Content

Break down the video into scenes and state what will be covered in each scene. You will attach a completed script later.

IV. Production Format

What kind of video will this be—educational, documentary, humorous, or dramatic?

KidVid, © 2000 Zephyr Press, Tucson, Arizona.

A. Summarize in a short paragraph the intended plot of your video. Include a description of setting and mood.

B. List by character name each character in the script, along with a short description of that character's physical appearance and personality.

C. List the materials you need for your video: audio (sound), staging (set), lighting, graphics, or special props? Include a complete script and a floor plan of the set if necessary.

V. Budget

Consider your needs for materials, space, equipment, and people. Submit as real a budget as possible. Talk to your teacher about what the school can provide.

VI. Evaluation

What recommendations do you have for measuring the success of your video with your intended audience?

This Video Production Proposal is due before you begin production. It will be evaluated on originality, creativity, and practicality as well as on quality of thought, neatness, spelling, grammar, and promptness. It can be word processed or printed neatly.

KidVid, © 2000 Zephyr Press, Tucson, Arizona.

Appendix J
OPTIONAL LESSON:
PROCESS VIDEO
Teacher's Objectives

- to explain what *process video* is
- to help students become aware of *video trance*
- to help students make and analyze a process video

STUDENTS' OBJECTIVES

- to identify *process video*
- to recognize the viewing habits associated with commercial television and process video
- to recognize the dangers of *video trance*
- to make a process video and analyze it

FUNDAMENTALS

Process video is different from studio and commercial television in that it is the immediate and direct recording of a live, unrehearsed event. Process video is a window through which we can view how we act with others. Looking at real-life events through process video is an important antidote to commercial television, which is often out of touch with reality. No one who has watched commercial television will deny that the video images we see affect our behavior. We respond not only to what we recognize as *information* but to other aspects as well, aspects that we do not always recognize—a fact well known in marketing research. Evidence is increasing, for example, that violence on television teaches us to engage in violent behavior, even though we don't set out to learn it.

Process video is used by trainers, professionals, therapists, and others seeking to help people work and relate more effectively. It helps people to see their behavior as others see it and reinforce what is positive and change what is not.

In process video, an event is recorded exactly as it happens. There is no staging, no studio, no prepared script. Process video is straightforward and easy to do. Students can record a school project, a guest presentation, a classroom discussion. Just turn on the camera and roll tape!

The important part of process video is what happens after the recording. In process video, we see ourselves and others clearly. We see how we act and react with those around us. Process video is an important learning tool. But schooled for years by commercial television, we often must be taught to view process video effectively.

Commercial television strongly influences our viewing habits, not only what we see but how we see it. Our acquired viewing habits frequently interfere with our ability to learn from process video. As a result, it is usually necessary to structure the viewing process so that students can overcome habits acquired through years of viewing commercial television.

Video Trance

The most obvious and serious barrier to learning from process video is *video trance*. Watching television is such a passive activity that most people are unprepared to react spontaneously to video material. Most of us watch television as a form of relaxation, and we are accustomed to having our attention drawn to events rather than directing our attention ourselves. We need to actively scan, search, track, and discuss what we see in process video. Commercial television producers, well aware of video trance, attract attention at key points with sounds, music, changes in volume, flashes, crashes, sexual imagery, unexpected events, visual distortions, and a variety of other techniques. As a result, many viewers face the television or video monitor and expect to be spoon fed.

Breaking Barriers to Learning

Do not be discouraged if students seem disinterested or unwilling to invest any energy in learning from process video. You are probably seeing the overt signs of video trance. You can disrupt it in several ways:

Identify the Problem. Before beginning to study process video, describe video trance. Many students are better able to maintain their vigilance once they are aware of the problem.

Break It Up. The attention span for this kind of video material runs between five and ten minutes for untrained viewers. Keep it short and you'll keep your audience. Most process videos are not viewed from start to finish. A segment is often preselected to stimulate discussion.

Guide Discussion. Briefly tell students what they will see in the pre-selected video segment. Because commercial television highlights the "message" so clearly, most viewers are not prepared to absorb all the information in a video. Direct students' attention to significant details. If possible, stand beside the monitor and point out important events. A remote control is almost essential for viewing process video effectively. Help students scan the total picture. Events in the background may be just as relevant as events in the foreground. Ask students to search the total picture for important events. Ask them to track important people and activities. Tracking is the ability to follow people or activities even though they move about in the picture, come in and out of focus, or recede into the background. A videographer cannot always follow a significant activity and keep it in focus. Help students track important people or events by standing beside the monitor and pointing them out.

Discussion. You can reduce the passivity of video trance by talking about the video material segment by segment. Ask students to comment on what they see. Many such comments are critical. Ask students for alternative approaches and ideas. Viewers learn from the discussion as well as from the video. In many learning situations, the video is used mainly to stimulate discussion prior to solving a problem or making a decision. Discussion also lets you measure what students are getting from the tape—can they observe accurately and reconstruct events that they have seen?

Repeat it. Use your remote control (or search dial if your machine has one) to repeat and review material. Fast forwarding or rewinding allows students to review certain segments immediately.

Substance vs. Appearance

Commercial television is partially responsible for our fixation on appearance—clothing, hair, makeup. When you see yourself on video for the first time, it is typical to get caught up in your appearance. It helps to talk about this phenomenon in advance and discuss with your students what process video is really all about—substance. We are not looking at how we appear. We are looking at how we behave, particularly in collaboration with others.

THE TEACHER WILL NEED TO KNOW

- what process video is

MATERIALS

- a short process video (for example, a tape of a classroom discussion)
- a taped television commercial
- a VCR and television
- a remote control for the VCR

VOCABULARY

Process video
Scan
Search
Track
Video trance

PROCEDURES

Preparation: Ask students if they ever got so involved in a television program that they failed to hear or see things around them. After students share their experiences, discuss the advantages and disadvantages of this experience. Explain that today's lesson will give them new ways to deal with it.

1. Define *video trance*. Ask students to describe their experience with video trance. Tell them that in contrast to commercial television, process video is like looking through a window at how we learn. (We're teaching and learning all the time, although it's not formally recognized.)

2. Television vs. process video. Review a segment of a rental movie, television show, or television commercial for the techniques used to attract our attention. Ask students to contrast these segments with real life. Ask them to list these comparisons. For example, do police shoot their guns every day? Most do only a few times in their career.

3. Review process video. Review with students the process video you have made. Guide their observation. Use the vocabulary *scan, search,* and *track.* Discuss with them what they see.

4. Videotape a school project. If you do not have a process videotape, ask students to tape a school project to learn more about process. Or give students the camera and ask them to tape you teaching the class or peer helper activities. The idea is for the camera to look at the teaching and the learning to discover which methods work and which do not. Encourage students to review the tapes and scan, search, track, and discuss. Tape the same activity on another day and discuss it again.

5. Videotape a student discussion. Ask students to tape their discussion of a process video segment and then review the discussion. Always remember that the focus is on learning and finding out what methods are most effective. Remind students that this is the goal of process video. For example, "Look, Mark's beginning to share his ideas in discussion. And Joanne is listening more and letting others talk. Steve gave a nice explanation of where the nurse is to that new student." Discussions of process video should always have a positive focus.

6. Evaluate your process video session. Ask students what they have learned about process video. Ask for new examples of how students could use process video.

7. Homework. For extra credit, students can take home a process video segment and share it with their parents.

8. Share it with the principal. Ask students to share a process video with the principal. Ask them to do a trial run with you first. Help them design their presentation. You could even videotape the presentation.

9. Process video in the school. Let it be known that your class is available to make process videotapes to be used in school. Suggest that your students practice presenting the finished process video to the people involved and guiding discussion.

Appendix K
OPTIONAL LESSON: ARTISTIC VIDEO
Objective

- To practice skills of elaboration, fluency, and flexibility in the creation of an artistic video

Discuss with the students the ways in which artists often take ordinary things and, by changing the mood, setting, theme, characters, or plot, create something new.

Share with students artistic books or videos that show things from various perspectives or that show elements used in original and unique ways (dancing hands, talking animals, and so on). Discuss the videos or books. What different effects did the creators use (music, lighting, makeup, props, movement, sets)? How did the creator use these techniques to create effects? What is an effect? Are effects good or bad? When are they good or bad? What other effects have students seen?

Assignment

Students work in groups of no more than three to produce an original artistic video of no more than three minutes. The video must take an ordinary object and manipulate, move, or show it in a different angle or light. They have one week in class to create their videotapes.

Students may use lighting effects, music, and other elements, but they must provide their own equipment (for example, flashlights, CDs, or audiotapes). You may want to supply red, black, white, sky blue, or yellow backdrop paper.

Each team selects a producer and director. Teams may begin working on their scripts immediately to plan to tape the week after the assignment is given.

Each student on the team must appear in the video. Each student must use the camera at some time. The team will create a title and credits to show in the video.

Appendix L
EVALUATING VIDEOS: CONTENT STANDARDS AND QUALITY
Content Standards

Video production requires skill, not a knowledge of specific content. It is most effective when used to illustrate knowledge of a content area or as a culminating activity for a unit. Therefore, your evaluation of students' content acquisition will be as individual as your teaching method. You will need to establish your goals and objectives ahead of time and communicate them clearly.

It's difficult to generalize because there are so many different standards, rubrics, and scoring guides that teachers are expected to follow.

Assuming you understand your particular guidelines, your evaluation should allow for a continuum of concept acquisition as well as skill development. You should tailor your rubric for your given activity and class understandings. Lewin and Shoemaker (1998) give guidelines for the characteristics of various steps on the content continuum:

Stage 1: Not Present
Student presents no information about the subject and makes no attempt to address the subject in any meaningful way.

Stage 2: Ready
Student makes an attempt to address the subject but provides no detail; no breadth of information is present.

Stage 3: Beginning
Student has a narrow frame of reference and uninformed opinions. She gives irrelevant, simplistic, or inaccurate information.

Stage 4: Developing
Student gives some relevant and accurate information based on fact as well as increasingly informed opinion. His argument is weak or implausible. He identifies central issues but states them in general terms.

Stage 5: Progressing
Student shows comprehension of pertinent facts and concepts by drawing data from a variety of primary and secondary sources. She demonstrates a rudimentary understanding of related principles, laws, and theorems, and uses the information to solve simple problems.

Stage 6: Accomplished
Student presents a breadth and depth of relevant and accurate facts, concepts, and generalizations applicable to the subject. He investigates the subject through an analysis of its parts and presents multiple appropriate perspectives, supporting those perspectives. He begins to show original thinking in approaching and presenting data.

Stage 7: Expert
Student focuses on substantive themes, problems, and issues. She evaluates information related to the subject, and makes quantitative and qualitative judgments about the subject. She synthesizes and extends facts, concepts, and generalizations about the subject; presents acquired knowledge in a number of different forms from concrete to abstract; and shows original thinking and creativity in approaching and presenting the data.

Your final evaluation should allow content to be presented accurately and thoroughly enough to indicate understanding with appropriate detail. You may want to use a sliding scale in your rubric to evaluate each area.

Quality of Video

As mentioned earlier, a high-quality video requires skill. When evaluating skills, define the level of expectation as clearly as possible, then focus on the level of expertise displayed. Differentiate between the skills used and the content level expressed: a student could create a great script that does not represent a deep understanding of the content. That's why you need the Production Proposal: it defines the audience and establishes student awareness of evaluation criteria ahead of time.

Video Production Checklist

An individual or group can do an assessment of any product, and the assessment can be either product or process oriented. It's important that you state your goals clearly at the beginning of the project and restate them when the project is complete, before beginning the evaluation. I have used this checklist to evaluate student-created videos. Since the students in the class decided to work in small groups, I used a multipurpose evaluation form. Students completed individual self-evaluations, then evaluated each member of their teams, ending with the producers and directors. I averaged the scores and comments and added my own evaluation, then transferred that information to another copy that the student received as a final, composite grade. This process ensured anonymity and tended to water down any personal grudges or favoritism that could have resulted in unfairly low or high grades. Team members stated their overall satisfaction with their video, then evaluated one another's individual contributions to the planning, the production, and the finished product. You can also use this checklist as a progress report at intervals throughout production.

GLOSSARY

Audience: everyone who will view a particular videotape

Audio: the sound portion of a videotape, usually found on two tracks

Audio dub: to record sound only, without disturbing the picture portion of a videotape; sometimes dubbed on one track only, preserving the original sound on the other track

Audio head: the magnetic recording head that records or plays back sound

Audio in: a sound input connection for incoming sound signals

Audio out: a sound output connection for outgoing sound signals

Backlight: on a video set, a light coming from behind the subject

Bouncing light: a technique that uses a white surface to reflect light to fill in harsh shadows

Cable: a wire carrying video and/or audio signals from one piece of equipment to another

Camcorder: a video camera that records directly onto an inserted videotape

Characterizations: the physical and psychological profiles of characters

Close-up (CU): a camera shot in which an object or part of an object is seen at close range or framed tightly

Criteria: the standards on which a judgment is based

"Cut": the director's cue to stop the recording

Director: in a video production, the person responsible for the script, storyboard, camera shots, and all other day-to-day activities

Documentary: a video treatment that presents a subject for historical purposes

Dolly: the wheeled frame on which a tripod sits

Dolly in or out: to move the camera forward or back on its wheeled frame

Dramatic: a video treatment that dramatizes some fictional or nonfictional story

Dub: to copy all or part of a video program from one videotape to another

Edit: to select and electronically assemble two or more audio and video segments into a single program

Educational: a video treatment that demonstrates how something works, presents factual informational, or describes something

Extreme close-up (ECU): a very close camera shot

Fade: in audio, to decrease in volume; in video, to make the picture go gradually black ("fade out") or appear gradually on screen from black ("fade in")

Fill light: on a video set, an artificial light used to fill in shadows

Focal length: the distance between the camera lens and the recording surface

Focus: the clarity of the picture

Generation loss: the successive reduction of video quality that occurs during dubbing

Graphics: any written or drawn material used on camera

Head: the electromagnetic device that records or retrieves information from magnetic tape

Head room: the space between the top of the screen and the object in the frame

Humorous: a video treatment that seeks to make people laugh

Jump cut: when a picture obviously skips from shot to shot or skips intermediate action

Key spot: on a video set, the main light

Layering: in constructing a video, the deliberate choice of varying elements to appeal to a variety of audiences

Lens: an optical lens, necessary for perceiving an image

Line in: an audio or video input point from other equipment

Line out: an audio or video output point to other equipment

Lip sync: an instance in which the picture of a person's lips moving matches the sound of his or her voice

Log: to watch a videotape and make an inventory of the various recorded scenes on it

Long shot (LS): a camera shot that includes a large field of view

Medium shot (MS): a camera shot that shows a person from the waist up or about half an object and some background

Monitor/receiver: a dual-function standard television receiver and monitor that receives and transmits audio and video signals

Mood: the tone of the production, such as humorous, dramatic, fantastic, or introspective

Pan: to pivot the camera from side to side

Plot: the story line of the work

Point of view: the perspective taken in a video production

Postproduction: usually refers to the editing process

Preproduction: the planning stage of any production (includes script writing, research, scheduling, and budget planning)

Process video: videotaping that records a live, unrehearsed action

Producer: in a video production, the person responsible for the content, audience, and objectives of the production

Ready cue: the director's signal to talent and crew that taping is imminent

"Roll tape": the director's cue for the cameraperson to begin recording

Roll time: the 5-count interval in which the videotape is rolling but the action has not yet begun

Scan: in viewing process video, to review the video frame quickly for important elements in both the foreground and background

Scoop light: inexpensive clip-on lights with a single bulb and metal casing

Search: in viewing process video, to look for important people or events in each frame

Setting: the location in place and time in which the work occurs

Special effects: transitional effects (such as wipes, fades, or dissolves) or complementary effects (such as titles); also describes digitally produced effects (such as picture flips)

"Stand by": the director's cue that videotaping is imminent

Studio video: videotaping that occurs in a controlled studio setting

Sync: shortened form of *synchronization;* the timing pulses that keep television scanning circuits working together

Take: the recording of a single shot or scene

Talent: in a video production, the people who appear on camera

"Tape rolling": the cameraperson's response to tell the director that videotape recording has begun

Teamwork: in a video production, the result of all crewmembers respecting the hierarchy of authority and working together effectively

Theme: the overall idea for a work

Tilt: a camera shot that points the camera up or down

Time Cues "5, 4, 3, 2, 1": the director's cues that the action will begin in 5 counts

Titles: any graphic material shown on camera

Track: in viewing process video, to follow important people or events throughout the entire videotape

Tracking: an electronic alignment of the video heads so that what is played back matches what was recorded, giving a clearer picture

Treatment: the manner in which the subject of a video production is portrayed

Truck: to move the camera left or right to follow the subject

Two-shot: framing two people or objects with the camera lens

Video: the picture portion of a videotape

Video in: a video input point from other equipment

Video out: a video output point to other equipment

Videotape: magnetic tape that can record a television signal

Video trance: the passive manner in which most people have learned to watch commercial television

"You're on" (action): the director's cue to talent to begin the action

Zoom: the gradual changing of the focal length of the lens, giving the effect of dollying without moving the camera, accomplished by pressing the camera's zoom toggle button

Zoom in: using the lens to give the effect of moving closer to the subject

Zoom out: using the lens to give the effect of moving away from the subject

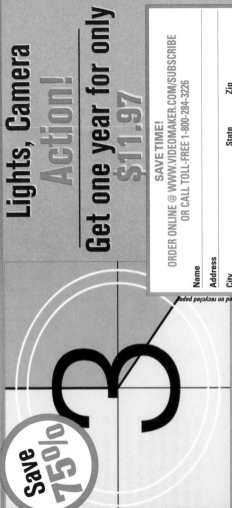

BUSINESS REPLY MAIL

FIRST-CLASS MAIL   PERMIT NO. 755   CHICO CA

POSTAGE WILL BE PAID BY ADDRESSEE

Videomaker

PO BOX 3780
CHICO CA 95927-9840

INTERNET RESOURCES

www.aect.org/

The website for the Association for Educational Communications and Technology, which is dedicated to "facilitat[ing] humane learning through the systematic development, utilization, and management of learning resources, which include people, processes and media in educational settings"

www.cme.org/

The website for the Center for Media Education, a national nonprofit organization dedicated to improving the quality of electronic media, especially on behalf of children and their families

www.kqed.org/cel/school/mediaclassroom/videoprod/manual.html

A web resource guide for teachers that addresses some of the main areas concerning video production in the classroom

www. scriptorama.com/

A website that links you to hundreds of scripts from movies and TV shows; an exciting way to show your students "real" work! (Be sure to peruse it first and supervise students—all kinds of shows are on this, if you know what I mean!)

www.schoolTV.com./

A great website reference with lots of information; numerous links to other sites as well

www.videomaker.com/

One of the best online magazines in video production

BIBLIOGRAPHY

Bryant, Steve. 1994. *Basic Camcorder Guide.* Amherst, N.Y.: Amherst Media.

Caputo, Linda. 1986. *Write, Camera, Action!* Santa Barbara, Calif.: The Learning Works.

Lewin, Larry, and Betty Jean Shoemaker. 1998. *Great Performances: Creating Classroom Based Assessment Tasks.* Alexandria, Va.: Association for Supervision and Curriculum Development.

Millerson, Gerald. 1992. *Video Production Handbook.* London: Focal Press.

Schroeppel, Tom. 1982. *The Bare Bones Camera Course for Film and Video.* Tampa, Fla.: Tom Schroeppel.

Stavros, Michael. 1995. *Camcorder Tricks and Special Effects.* Amherst, N.Y.: Amherst Media.

About the Author

Kaye Black teaches and designs curriculum for middle school students at Brady Middle School in the Orange, Ohio, School District. She developed *KidVid* while teaching a filmmaking unit and in response to requests from teachers and administrators for materials and inservice instruction.

Kaye received a B.S. in elementary and gifted education and an M.Ed. in gifted education from Kent State University. In 1997 she achieved National Board Certification in the area of Middle Childhood/Generalist. She continues to present and work with teachers and National Board candidates all over the country. She was recently chosen to serve on the selection panel for the Walt Disney Teacher of the Year Awards.

In addition to teaching, Kaye enjoys acting in theater and musical productions, both amateur and professional.

Zephyr
Press ®
REACHING THEIR HIGHEST POTENTIAL

P.O. Box 66006
Tucson, Arizona 85728-6006

Motivate Students to Learn through Movement and Other Fun Activities

You'll find movement experiences so motivating that you'll ask for more

MORE MOVING EXPERIENCES
Connecting Arts, Feelings, and Imagination
by Teresa Benzwie, Ed.D.; illustrated by Robert Bender

Grades K–12+

Foster the imagination essential to the learning process with expressive move-ment experiences. Learn how to create experiences that allow your students to concentrate, problem solve, and develop self-awareness.

Get students of all ages and abilities into action with activities based on dance therapy techniques. Select from more than 180 activities that encourage a bodily-kinesthetic and intrapersonal understanding of a wide spectrum of concepts. Activities can be done individually or in groups. Includes—

- Learning about me—writing and movement, art
- Dancing the web—body awareness, guided visualization
- Sequencing—telling a story, all about me
- Nonverbal communication—mirroring, yes-no dance
- And many more

1062-W . . . $29

Use rhythm to optimize learning in the classroom

RAPPIN' AND RHYMIN'
Raps, Songs, Cheers, and SmartRope Jingles for Active Learning
by Rosella R. Wallace, Ph.D.

Grades K–8

This book and tape set uses the powers of rhythm and rhyme to teach children the information they need to know in a way they want to learn. With *Rappin' and Rhymin'* you can—

- Motivate student participation
- Engage students in large-group response activities
- Enhance learning by providing enrichment and joy, and relieving stress
- Optimize learning—at home and in the classroom

73-page activity manual and 20-minute audiotape
1028-W . . . $27

Teach basic classroom facts fast with this fun, stress-free approach

SMARTROPE JINGLES
Jump Rope Rhymes, Raps, and Chants for Active Learning
by Rosella R. Wallace, Ph.D.

Grades 3–9

With these rhymes and chants, you can teach your students more and increase their recall dramatically. This one-of-a-kind collection can be used to teach—

- Multiplication tables
- State capitals
- Planets of our solar system
- Roman numerals

Teachers and parents have used these chants and raps with children in the classroom, in special education programs, in ESL, on the playground, in P.E., and at home.

91-page activity manual and 30-minute audiotape
1916-W . . . $27

Boost your students' learning with 88 stimulating activities

EVERY BODY CAN LEARN
Engaging the Bodily-Kinesthetic Intelligence in the Everyday Classroom
by Marilyn Nikimaa Patterson, M.A.

Grades 5–12

Make teaching easier and more effective by using kinesthetic activities in your classroom. Combine this approach with traditional methods of teaching to help middle and high school students—

- Get a more complete picture of any subject
- Reduce inhibitions to learning
- Produce long-term recall

A helpful cross-referenced chart shows you the range of subjects appropriate for each of the 88 activities. Plus, you'll get a valuable resource guide. You'll also have well-defined activities for English and other languages, social sciences, mathematics, and natural sciences.

1078-W . . . $30

BRAIN FOOD

Games That Make Kids Think

by Paul Fleisher, M.Ed.

Grades 4–12+

Be the one to make a difference in your students' thinking! With more than 100 games to choose from, *Brain Food* is your one-stop source for exploring the fun in learning. This compilation is filled with new as well as traditional games, and most need little more than paper and pencil to get you started. Each game is classroom tested and tailored to enhance the intelligences of your students. You'll find—

- 70 reproducible game boards
- More than 100 word, logical, mathematical, and strategic games
- A multicultural selection of games from places as varied as Africa, Denmark, New Zealand, and Indonesia

1088-W . . . $36

Your students will remember their multiplication tables with the power of stories, music, and rhythm—all in one complete program!

ELLA VANILLA'S MULTIPLICATION SECRETS

Building Math Memory with Rhythm and Rhyme

by Rosella R. Wallace, Ph.D.

Grades K–8

This complete program gives you 13 delightful stories about Ella Vanilla's adventures. Plus, you'll have a musical tape reinforcing the raps presented in the stories. Your students will—

- Learn raps and rhymes about the multiplication tables
- Find out about math facts, fun, and fitness
- Explore choices, teamwork, and responsibility

This time-saving program has everything you need for presenting the lessons—

- 24 reproducible blacklines for making overheads
- 13 delightful stories about Ella Vanilla's adventures
- 30-minute audiotape to bring music into your lessons
- 12 reproducible games and work sheets for individual and group learning

120 pages in a 3-ring binder and a 30-minute audiotape

1085-W . . . $39